PROTECTING **YOUR**
MONEY, PRIVACY & IDENTITY FROM
THEFT, LOSS & MISUSE

PRACTICAL STEPS FOR TODAY'S WORLD!

Jim **Gaston**, FCA · Paul K. **Wing**, FCCA

National Library of Canada Cataloguing in Publication

Gaston, S. J. (Stephen James)

   Protecting your money, privacy and identity from theft, loss and misuse / Jim Gaston, Paul K. Wing.

ISBN 1-55385-021-1

   1. False personation—Prevention. 2. Internet fraud—Prevention. 3. Electronic commerce—Corrupt practices. I. Wing, Paul K. II. Canadian Institute of Chartered Accountants III. Title.

HV6675.G38 2003   364.16'3   C2003-903173-X

FOREWORD

The Information Age has created new ways of performing day-to-day tasks such as banking, shopping and communicating, and regardless of whether you are technically savvy with the latest electronic devices or still prefer to do business with a pen and paper, you are a participant.

But the Information Age has also created new opportunities for impersonation, eavesdropping, spying, theft and fraud. Although these crimes have existed for thousands of years, computers, the Internet, telephones, faxes, bankcards, and other devices have created new ways of committing these crimes, often from many kilometres away or from the opposite side of the globe.

Even if the only electronic device you use is the telephone, you are not immune to the possibility of being a victim. Your relationships with government, financial institutions, retailers, utility companies and your employer are recorded electronically and ensure that you could become a victim of the crimes described in **Protecting Your Money, Privacy and Identity from Theft, Loss and Misuse** — *Practical Steps for Today's World.*

Having worked in the computer industry for 20 years and computer security for 15 years, I have seen the personal computer go from relative obscurity to becoming a basic life skill; the growth of the Internet from being a tool used by a few to being one of the most valued tools today for communicating with family and friends; the development of the telephone from analog to digital to cellular; the video camera move from the movie set to the backyard; and the creation of Privacy Commissioners to protect your personal information from corporate and government misuse. Ever since electronic devices came into our lives, information security specialists have been challenged to keep pace with the threats that they introduce.

Protecting Your Money, Privacy and Identity from Theft, Loss and Misuse will allow you to learn from two people who are internationally recognized as information security and privacy specialists, who have worked with governments, businesses and financial institutions for many years identifying, testing and implementing the best ways to protect your information and your money. Paul and Jim have protected personal information from misuse, investigated card fraud, protected personal computers from viruses and tracked hackers across the Internet.

Until now, the onus has been on you to sort through banking agreements, brochures, media reports, user manuals, etc., to figure out how to protect your personal information from being stolen or misused, your personal computer from being hacked, your e-mail from being infected by a virus or your bankcard from being stolen. **Protecting Your Money, Privacy and Identity from Theft, Loss and Misuse** consolidates all of this information into one easy-to-read book without a lot of technical jargon, but lots of practical advice. The book explains when and how you can become a victim, what steps you can take to reduce that risk, and finally, in recognition that protection is never perfect, it explains what to do if you do become a victim.

Using even a few of the suggestions in this book will help you and your family have a safe passage through the Information Age. Enjoy the trip!

BEV EDWARDS

TABLE OF CONTENTS

1

PROTECTING YOUR
MONEY, PRIVACY AND IDENTITY

It's a typical day. You've used a credit card to enter a parking lot, used your cell phone to check your bank balances, sent several e-mails including one to order new cheque books, put the lunch tab on a credit card, ordered office supplies on the Internet and paid by credit card, faxed a credit card application that you downloaded from the Internet, paid for your dry cleaning with your debit card and mailed your application for a new passport. When you arrived home, you checked the mail and tossed an unsolicited, personally addressed credit application form into the recycle bin.

It's a typical day — and behind every one of these common activities may lurk the information thieves of the 21st century who can, without your knowledge, access and use your personal information to their advantage, and your loss.

The potential for injury and loss is part of each of your common everyday activities. It includes the documents you continuously carry in your wallet or purse, your physical mail and electronic mail, your use of the telephone, cell phone or fax, your bank and investment accounts and bankcards, your online banking and buying, and your disclosure of personal sensitive information whether face-to-face, over the telephone or online. Many people may routinely perform these common, everyday activities with little thought of the risks involved, whether at home, at work or study, or while travelling for business or pleasure. Others may simply avoid new technology, as they believe it is "too risky". While daily activities involving the Internet are increasingly common and even routine, many people may have little knowledge or understanding of the inherent risks.

The risks of these everyday activities are many and generally involve:
• A loss of privacy, where your personal information becomes available to others and might be used against you.
• Misinterpretation, where your personal information held by others is incorrect or misleading.
• Monetary losses, where fraudulent transactions drain your financial accounts, rack up debt and damage your credit rating.
• Theft, or hijacking of your identity where others masquerade and do business as if they were you (and not just on the Internet).

3

The risks of this Information Age are real — regardless of whether you use the Internet frequently, infrequently, or not at all. In fact, far more people suffer monetary losses because of credit or debit card fraud, or have their privacy invaded through means that have nothing to do with the Internet than those whose losses are directly attributable to the Internet. The Internet simply provides additional opportunities for criminal activities since people who communicate or do business over the Internet may never meet face to face. This trend of doing things with people you do not know and have never met, the faceless contact facilitated by the Internet, makes it much easier for an impostor to hijack your identity and successfully use it.

The goal of **Protecting Your Money, Privacy and Identity from Theft, Loss and Misuse — Practical Steps for Today's World** is to reduce the likelihood of you or members of your family becoming a victim of the Information Age and, where you consistently follow the advice, reduce the potential impact. If, despite these safeguards, you do become a victim, this book also provides the steps to take to clear up the problems that may arise, e.g., correct your credit record.

IDENTITY THEFT

The most insidious crime today is identity theft or hijacking and the number of reported incidents continue to rise each year. An identity thief can use your personal information to redirect mail, open credit card and financial accounts, enter into contracts and mortgages, rent vehicles, secure employment and carry out transactions in your name. The media reports how individuals may only learn of their identity being hijacked when contacted about a delinquent credit account for which they never applied — at which point their credit rating had already been severely damaged — and how the victims must then painstakingly clear up many fraudulent transactions.

UNDERSTANDING AND MINIMIZING YOUR RISKS

While there are no foolproof ways to totally prevent theft and losses, you can take practical and proactive steps to minimize your risks and reduce your exposure to losses and being a victim. Throughout this book, each chapter provides steps that you can take to ensure you have a fundamental level of control over your personal and financial information, and thus your privacy.

Low to High Risk
In addition, each chapter identifies the level of risk for the various exposures. Your risk may be low, moderate or high, depending on the nature of the specific activity, how you undertake the activity, and how often you do it.

Chapter 16 — Crisis Management provides approaches for dealing with personal information losses or accidents, and helps you recognize and manage identity theft so that you can minimize the potential impact on you and your family. The Resources section provides further guidance, tips and techniques that can help you reduce the risk of having your personal information accessed and misused.

This book is aimed at individuals in their everyday lives. It does not cover the additional challenges that businesses and professional practices face or the steps owner/managers and managing partners should take to protect a business or practice. These are subjects for another book.

PROVIDING INFORMATION TO OTHERS

When you provide information to a person, organization or Internet-based enterprise through a website, use a debit or credit card, use a cordless telephone, a cell phone, a personal digital assistant (PDA), use your personal computer or another computer, send or receive physical mail or e-mail, the risk of others accessing and misusing your most sensitive information is always present.

- Organizations gather personal data on their clients and, in turn, may share this information with other organizations.
- Employees of these companies can access, and potentially misuse, your personal data.
- Information thieves can eavesdrop on your cell phone calls, steal your mail, and in other ways gain information to masquerade as you.
- Internet hackers can intercept your e-mail or rifle your personal computer for folly or profit.

At the same time, private and public organizations tend to trust and act upon the information they have collected about you in their systems without further checking. If you discover an error, you may even be treated dismissively. Erroneous personal data has ever-increasing dire consequences, but when an error does happen, having it rectified may lead you through a maze of frustration.

As companies increasingly find new ways to give their customers what they want, when they want it, consumers have learned to expect instant gratification. Financial institutions let you withdraw money instantly at ABMs (automated banking machines) worldwide, credit cards provide on-the-spot loans, and the Internet allows purchases with the click of a mouse. Security and convenience are often opposing forces. The more security, the more inconvenience you must shoulder. The practical steps throughout this book, however, will help you protect yourself with relatively little inconvenience or personal cost. They are easy to follow and undoubtedly worth the effort.

ESSENTIAL LIFE SKILLS FOR THE INFORMATION AGE

Knowing ways to protect yourself in the Information Age and knowing how to travel the information highway knowledgeably and defensively are essential life skills today. The scope of these life skills includes a wide range of today's technology and your daily activities, whether you are using your bankcards worldwide to access your bank accounts at ABMs or on the Internet online from anywhere, at anytime.

The life skills everyone needs today are as fundamental as learning how to drive the vehicular highways — learning the rules of the road and taking measures to reduce the likelihood of an accident, yet knowing how to proceed if an accident does occur.

Consider how many years, accidents and losses it took from the time the car was invented before society began to take serious measures to educate and protect — teach traffic safety to children, raise safety standards for car manufacturing and road construction, equip cars with seat belts, air bags and other safety devices, crack down on impaired drivers, and take other measures to reduce risk and protect drivers, passengers and pedestrians alike. All of these measures emerged gradually and became more stringent as cars became more powerful, traffic more congested and accidents more frequent and more serious.

This analogy applies to the information highway you travel today. Society has entered an era of new risks that demands new methods for protecting yourself. Computers are more powerful, the accumulation of data and information on individuals continues to expand and travel far and wide, and more people are having their money absconded, their privacy and peace of mind invaded, and their identity hijacked — regardless of whether you travel the information highway as a driver, passenger or pedestrian.

Technological change is constant and the pace is only increasing. While many may try to avoid it, many others assume that newer technology is inherently safer, which is not necessarily the case. The life skills you need in today's world were not taught at school and in protecting your money, privacy and identity, it is not acceptable to learn from the "school of hard knocks" and bad experiences. This book is intended to improve your understanding and help you change your behaviours and develop some increasingly essential life skills.

PROTECTING YOURSELF IN TODAY'S WORLD

This book is as up-to-date as possible at press time, but technology and processes are rapidly changing. You need to constantly watch for new developments and changes. Recently the major banks introduced a service by which you can send money to others by e-mail and a major manufacturer has announced a new line of personal computers that contain security chips that help address certain risks. These and other developments will obviously change the risks you face and the steps you need to take to protect yourself in today's fast-changing world.

Society is only at the beginning stages of designing information "seat belts and air bags", building safer information vehicles, passing legislation and regulations to control information traffic and protect the individual's privacy, and teaching people the steps they can take to protect themselves. Even if you take every precaution — walk and drive defensively, know the rules of the road and faithfully fasten your seat belt each time you drive — accidents can and do happen.

While there are no measures that will guarantee your safety, **Protecting Your Money, Privacy and Identity from Theft, Loss and Misuse — Practical Steps for Today's World** will help you recognize and reduce your risks, limit the potential for damage and losses, and respond quickly and effectively if, despite these precautions, you are a victim. Of course, there are no measures that will guarantee that mishaps and accidents do not occur along the way — but while life offers no guarantees, the chapters that follow can make a difference in yours. This book can help prevent your becoming a victim. In the worse case scenario, it can help you limit the effect of a theft, loss or misuse of your personal information.

Contact the Authors at protectyourself@rogers.com

Jim and Paul welcome your suggestions, tips and stories. Please e-mail your comments to the authors at: protectyourself@rogers.com

PROTECTING SENSITIVE INFORMATION AT HOME AND AWAY

2

When people talk about fraud and identity theft, the computer and the Internet are often the first things that come to mind. In fact, the Internet is NOT a factor in the majority of fraud cases; most losses and cases of identity theft arise out of the simple and mundane activities that are part of daily life. The thief who is intent on stealing your money, invading your privacy or hijacking your identity can obtain much of the required information through the relatively simple acts of stealing your wallet or your mail or rifling your sensitive documents in your home or workplace.

Of course, computer users must also consider the risks of an intruder accessing the files on a computer or intercepting their Internet transmissions to obtain their personal information. These risks and the practical steps you need to take are discussed later in Chapters 9 to 15 of this book.

YOUR WALLET

Whether you carry your wallet in your pocket or purse, it contains a wealth of information that a thief could use to advantage.

Low to High Risk

To reduce the potential losses if your wallet is lost or stolen, minimize the nature and amount of information you carry in your wallet.

PRACTICAL STEPS TO PROTECT YOURSELF
Protecting Information Carried in Your Wallet or Purse

- Carry only the credit cards and papers that you routinely use day-to-day. Carry your SIN card, birth certificate, passport or other documents you use occasionally only on those days that you need them.
- Always sign your personal identity documents and cards immediately upon receipt, such as your debit and credit cards, driver's licence and health card.
- Never leave your wallet or purse untended at your place of work or study, in your car, or in a hotel room. If you cannot keep it with you, lock it up.

- When a credit card or debit card is returned to you after a transaction, check to make sure it is your own card before returning it to your wallet. Cards can get switched, particularly where the processing is out of your sight, such as in a restaurant.
- If you lose your wallet, immediately report the loss to the police, your financial services institution and the government department that issued your various cards and documents. The importance of having a Quick Contact List is discussed later in this chapter.
- Immediately notify your financial services institution if your debit or credit card is lost or stolen or retained by an automated banking machine (ABM).

PERSONAL DIGITAL ASSISTANTS (PDAs)

If you use a personal digital assistant (PDA), such as Palm and iPAQ, this is also a source of personal information that you need to take steps to protect. The precautions for protecting your personal information in your wallet are just as applicable to these devices.

Moderate to High Risk

PDAs can present a high risk simply because they are small and easily lost or stolen. If you store your financial account numbers, social insurance number (SIN), passwords, and other sensitive information in your PDA, anyone that has access to it could access and use this information. To protect your privacy and identity, take the same precautions with a PDA that you would for your wallet.

PRACTICAL STEPS TO PROTECT YOURSELF
Protecting Personal Information on a PDA

- Do NOT store sensitive personal and financial information in your PDA.
- Do store your emergency contact numbers in your PDA but do NOT store debit or credit card numbers or PINs.
- Use password protection to prevent access to the information stored in your PDA.
- Safeguard your PDA at all times. Keep it in your possession. Do not leave it unattended at any time.

YOUR MAIL

Many items that arrive in your physical mailbox could be used to steal your money, invade your privacy or hijack your identity. Consider some of the items that may arrive in the mail:

- Credit card statements
- New bankcards — debit and credit cards and sometimes a personal identification number (PIN)
- Driver's licences
- Health cards
- Financial services account statements, which may include your cancelled cheques with your signature on them
- New chequebooks
- Statements from your investment or insurance brokers
- Telephone and cell phone bills
- Telephone calling cards
- Income tax assessments and other tax-related information, and
- Passports.

Low to High Risk

A thief can use the information found in your mail to masquerade as you, such as apply for a loan or a driver's licence. The thief does not have to steal many letters from your mailbox. With just two or three stolen documents, the thief may be able to have the post office forward your mail elsewhere and gather enough documents to carry out fraudulent transactions in your name.

PRACTICAL STEPS TO PROTECT YOURSELF
Protecting Your Mail

- If you have home delivery, install a mailbox in your door so that mail cannot be easily stolen. A thief can easily access an outside mailbox.
- If your mail is delivered to a community mailbox on the street or in a common area of an apartment or condominium building, empty your mailbox daily. Keep in mind that your mail is more likely to be stolen at night than during the day.
- When you are away for an extended period of time, arrange to have a trustworthy person empty your mailbox regularly and keep the contents in a safe place until your return.

- Before you open your mail, always do a visual check to see if there are signs of tampering. The person intent on stealing your identity may remove mail to retrieve personal data and then return the envelope intact to your mailbox. If any mail appears to have been tampered with, this could be an indication that someone is trying to steal your identity.
- Be acutely aware of the dates when you should be receiving important documents in the mail. Often, an organization can give you a timeframe as to when an item should arrive. If not, ask when you can expect to receive a particular document or statement. Write a reminder on your calendar or day planner and, if it does not arrive by that date, contact the sender immediately.
- Promptly follow up on items you are expecting and have not received, e.g., a new driver's licence, new chequebooks or credit card renewal.
- Be aware of the cycle in which you receive your family's most sensitive statements and accounts, such as your financial services statements or credit card statements. If not received when routinely expected, promptly follow up with the sender.
- In higher risk circumstances, such as having a community mailbox, you should consider requesting that certain items not be sent to you in the mail and arrange to pick these up in person. Pick up a renewal credit card, account statement or package of new cheques at your financial services branch. Pick up your driver's licence or passport from the issuer. Alternatively, ask if these items can be sent by registered mail so that you can pick them up at the post office.
- Carefully follow the instructions to activate any new or renewed personal identity document or cards, such as contacting your financial services institution to activate your credit card or removing a temporary sticker on a card.
- Sign your personal identity documents and cards immediately upon receipt, where a signature is required.

Taking Extra Precautions When Moving to Another Home
- Give direct notice of your change of address to your financial services institution and others who send sensitive personal information rather than depend on the post office's forwarding services.
- Promptly follow up on any mail that does not arrive when expected.

YOUR HOME AND WORKPLACE

Most people take measures to protect the valuables in their homes, such as locking doors, securing windows, carrying insurance coverage for losses from burglary and other risks and installing a security alarm system. But also consider that many documents and other sensitive sources of information in your home and the places where you work or study could be used to steal your money, invade your privacy or hijack your identity.

In familiar and comfortable places, people can be complacent about leaving personal items lying around — a wallet, purse, mail, bank statements, brokerage, mortgage, loan or credit card statements, utility bills, passports, tax records, the keys to the safe or mailbox and items recently received in the mail but not yet processed.

Moderate to High Risk

These are all potential sources for information about your identity and finances, items that can be used to access your bankcards or credit accounts, to assume your identity, to take over your telephone banking... to become you.

Part of your assessment of your risk exposure is to consider who has access to these familiar places and thus who could have access to your most sensitive information. Crime experts say it is often someone the victim knows who commits these crimes. Consider not only family members and close friends, but also visitors to your home such as guests, your children's friends, babysitters, housekeepers, cleaning service, workmen, and people attending a meeting held at your home. Consider the many people who access your workplace or school. Wallets, purses, knapsacks, computers and other personal items can disappear, even where the building is secured with security guards and electronic access cards.

PRACTICAL STEPS TO PROTECT YOURSELF

Protecting Your Personal Information at Home and at Your Workplace

- Store all sensitive and personal documents in a secure or well-hidden place that thieves cannot easily find or access, such as in a locked desk drawer.
- Store the most sensitive items in a safety deposit box or install a safe in your home for protecting these items.
- When providing the police with a list of the missing items after a burglary or robbery, be sure to include documents or sources of personal information that may have been taken. The Quick Contact List discussed below is your checklist for immediate action.

- After a burglary or robbery, be on high alert for symptoms or indications that your identity may be under attack. Identity theft is discussed in detail in Chapter 16 of this book, together with how you should proceed if you suspect or know you are a victim.

TAKING QUICK ACTION IN AN EMERGENCY

You suddenly discover your wallet or purse is missing. Do you have quick access to all the information it contained? Who do you contact to cancel debit and credit cards? How can you recover important documents that were lost? What if you later discover that someone is accessing your personal information and money, or in the "worst case" scenario, that you are a victim of identity theft?

Just as people know the importance of preparing a will and keeping it in a safe place, everyone needs to keep a current record of personal information that can be used in the event of crisis. This simple record is something everyone should complete and keep safe; however, few people ever get around to actually doing it.

Every person needs to prepare two emergency information lists:
- **Quick Contact List** – general contact information to carry with you.
- **Personal Information List** – a record of your sensitive personal information that must be kept in a very secure place.

These two lists are your first step for taking quick action in an emergency and dealing with the specific documents that have been lost or stolen. (Chapter 16 – Crisis Management details the other steps you need to take). Both of these lists are very important resources if you have reason to believe that someone has stolen your identity and is masquerading as you generally, and not just using a stolen card or document to steal money, misuse credit or forge or cash cheques.

THE QUICK CONTACT LIST

The *Quick Contact List* is your resource for immediately reporting lost or stolen items and preventing or limiting your losses. This list includes a concise record of the contact information that you will need in an emergency, such as discovering your wallet is missing. The information that you record on this list is largely public and not the sensitive personal information that others could use to harm you if it is found or stolen. You may also want to include the appropriate information for your spouse or partner and children.

A Sample Quick Contact List

CONTACT INFORMATION FOR:	Telephone #s from Home	In Canada	Outside North America	Date Checked
Financial Services Institution — Contact name				
Primary Credit Card				
Secondary Credit Card				
Store Card (name)				
Gas Token (name) Device				
Home Alarm Company				
Birth Certificate				
SIN Card				
Health Card				
Passport Date/Place of Issue				
Spouse's/Partner's Passport Date/Place of Issue				
Driver's Licence				
Car Insurance Company — Contact & Policy #				
House Insurance Company — Contact & Policy #				
Medical Insurance Company — Contact & Policy #				
ISP Dial-up				
Children's School				
Bell Canada Directory Assistance				
Identity Theft Notification — Credit Bureaus				
Police				
PhoneBusters[1]				

[1] PhoneBusters is the central agency in Canada that collects and disseminates information on identity theft complaints and facilitates prosecution. For more information, go to www.phonebusters.com

Record Minimal Contact Information

Note that the *Quick Contact List* includes only the minimum information that you need for taking immediate action in a crisis. Do NOT record the account or reference numbers of your credit and debit cards, passport or driver's licence numbers and other sensitive information on this list. List only the contact information that you would need if these items were lost or stolen. You may want to note the website addresses of places such as your financial services institution, as these are also helpful for contacting providers in an emergency, particularly if you are outside Canada when you need help.

Carry this List with You

Keep your *Quick Contact List* in your wallet. Make additional copies to keep in places such as in your car and day planner and with your passport and give a copy to a family member or friend. If you use an electronic organizer or PDA (personal digital assistant), you could also enter this information there. In addition, consider programming the contact emergency phone numbers into your home and office telephones and cell phone.

PERSONAL INFORMATION LIST

The *Personal Information List* is a master list on which you should record the very sensitive personal information that expands on the limited contact information you have recorded on your *Quick Contact List*. The *Personal Information List* is a much longer list than the *Quick Contact List*, as you include specific details such as account numbers in addition to the contact information you would need to access in an emergency. While the sample list below includes a great deal of information, you will likely need to record additional information as you customize it. You may also want to include the appropriate information for your spouse or partner and children.

A Sample Personal Information List

CONTACT INFORMATION FOR:	Telephone #s from Home	In Canada	Outside North America	Date Checked
Financial Services Institution — Contact Account # 1 Account # 2 Debit Card #				
Primary Credit Card — Acct #				
Secondary Credit Card — Acct #				
Store Card (name) — Acct #				
Store Card (name) — Acct #				
Gas Card (name) — Acct #				
Gas Token (name) Device — Acct #				
Home Alarm Company (name)				
Birth Certificate # Spouse's/Partner's #				
Citizenship Card # Spouse's/Partner's #				
SIN # Or Senior's Card # Spouse's/Partner's SIN #				
Provincial Health Card #				
Private Health Plan #				
Passport # Date and place of issue				
Spouse's/Partner's Passport # Date and place of issue				
Driver's Licence #				
Spouse's/Partner's Driver's Licence #				
Car Insurance Company — Contact & Policy #				
House Insurance Company — Contact & Policy #				
Medical Insurance Company — Contact & Policy #				

Low to High Risk

The *Personal Information List* must be kept in a very secure place, as it is a highly sensitive document.

PRACTICAL STEPS TO PROTECT YOURSELF
Using the Quick Contact and Personal Information Lists

- Take time to create a *Quick Contact List* and a *Personal Information List* as soon as possible. These records are a fundamental first step for protecting and managing your personal information.
- Store copies of the *Quick Contact List* in places where they can be quickly accessed in an emergency.
- Store the *Personal Information List* in a very secure place, such as in your home safe or a safety deposit box. This list contains information that would certainly put your money, privacy, and identity at risk if it were lost or stolen.
- Consider giving your lawyer a copy of the *Personal Information List* for safekeeping with your will. Do not make any other copies of this list.
- Remember to review and update your lists regularly to keep this information current.
- Consider making photocopies of the documents and cards that you have included on these lists, particularly those that you routinely carry in your wallet, and keep the photocopies safely with your *Personal Information List*.
- If you have elderly parents, encourage them to make these lists and provide you with copies for safekeeping.
- Many websites provide the contact information you need to record and update on your two lists, such as the specific government department for reporting a loss or requesting a replacement copy of a document.

EXTRA PRECAUTIONS FOR TRAVELLING

Global networks such as "PLUS" collect and exchange international automated banking machine (ABM) transactions from around the world. The logos or brands of the global networks to which your financial service institution subscribes are usually displayed on the back of your cards. These networks transport and clear the transactions, calculate the exchange rates, add any fees, set the security standards and settle the balances between the owner of the ABM that loaded the bills you withdrew and your financial services institution.

The security standards are vitally important as your debit or credit card number and PIN have to travel safely across a global network to your financial services institution to be verified as correct before cash is dispensed or a debit request transacted. As you do not want your card number and PIN travelling across this global network in plain text where others may access it, this identifying information must be encrypted. For this reason, you should only use the globally branded ABMs that are recommended and supported by your financial services provider as these provide secure transmissions.

Another safety measure is to only use an ABM that is located at a branch of a local major financial institution. This helps ensure physical safety and gives more assurance that the sticker indicating the machine is part of a major global network is real and not a forgery.

High Risk

Debit and credit card fraud are increasingly becoming international crimes. Cards issued by North American financial services institutions are particularly attractive to fraudsters because the credit limits tend to be higher than those of other countries.

When you travel, the consequences of having a credit card limit used up through fraudulent transactions or your financial accounts attacked using your debit card number and PIN can be much more severe than when you are in your own locale. Depending on where you are, it may be very difficult and time consuming to resolve matters and obtain replacement cards. You could be stranded without cash or credit.

Plan your trip carefully, take the proper precautions to reduce your risk exposures and have a back-up plan in case of an emergency.

PRACTICAL STEPS TO PROTECT YOURSELF
Taking Extra Precautions When Travelling

- Before you leave, update your *Quick Contact List,* discussed in this Chapter, to ensure you have the emergency contact toll-free and long distance telephone numbers for your financial services institution if you need to report that your debit or credit card is lost, stolen or retained by an ABM or need to transfer money to your account.
- Make several copies of your *Quick Contact List* for yourself and your travelling companions. Also leave a copy with a family member or friend in case you need this information in an emergency.

- Restrict the number of accounts linked to your debit or credit card so that your savings cannot be accessed with your debit card. Many online banking systems let you change the access to your accounts at a branded ABM machine.
- Reduce the balance on the linked financial account to an amount that is only sufficient for your trip. It may be safer to use a credit card for your purchases rather than a debit card while you are travelling.
- Ask your financial services institution to set a lower daily cash withdrawal limit on your debit card (or credit card if used for your ABM withdrawals). Your cash withdrawal limit affects the amount of cash you can withdraw within a 24-hour period. It does not affect your ability to pay in stores with your debit card.
- Change your PINs for your debit and/or credit cards before and after you travel to another country, particularly if you will be travelling outside North America. In effect, you should create a temporary PIN for duration of your trip. On your return, you can reinstate your previous PIN so it will be it easier to remember than a new PIN. Changing your PIN on your return ensures it can no longer be used if it has been compromised while you have been away.
- Plan to use only the globally branded ABMs recommended and supported by your financial services provider. Use only ABMs located at the branch of a local major financial institution. Be keenly aware of your surroundings when using an ABM in an unknown location.
- Use a "secondary" credit card to make hotel and car reservations and small routine purchases such as gas and long-distance telephone calls. You can still present and use your "primary" credit card when you check in at the hotel or pick up your rental car. See Chapter 4.
- Make sure your spouse or travelling companion carries a second credit card with a different number as a back-up or carry a second credit card yourself and keep it separate from your primary card, i.e., not in your wallet.

Booking and Staying at Hotels

When booking or staying at a hotel, consider the amount of personal information that the hotel's employees will collect and access. If you have made reservations, the hotel will already know your name, your home address, telephone number, credit card number, and perhaps your place of employment on your arrival. In some countries, you may be asked to provide your passport number when checking in. The hotel also knows when you plan to leave.

When you use your hotel room telephone, your personal calls will likely go through the hotel's central phone system or switchboard. What you discuss is one thing but consider the risk if you use your room telephone to do telephone banking. Someone with access to the hotel switchboard needs relatively little technical knowledge to be able to capture your bankcard number and access code.

If you plan to use your computer in your hotel room, you will likely need to dial up to your ISP. In this case, all of your online activity will also go through the hotel's telephone system or switchboard and the transmissions could be as accessible as a postcard.

Many hotel chains now offer wireless connectivity within their complex. Since the wireless network's radio waves are similar to those used for radio stations and cordless telephones, the transmissions could be potentially intercepted by anyone with the right kind of receiver on the same bandwidth. As discussed in Chapter 15, hotel staff or other guests in close proximity to your computer could hack into your wireless online communications without your knowledge.

Before you consider doing any personal computing from your hotel room, such as online banking, brokerage or purchasing, consider that others may be able to see your sensitive personal and financial information.

PRACTICAL STEPS TO PROTECT YOURSELF
Booking and Staying at Hotels

- Minimize the amount of personal information you give to a hotel on booking and at check in; for example, rather than provide your home address and telephone number, give your business address and telephone.
- Use discretion when tagging your luggage. Use only last name, and first initial along with your business address and telephone number, rather than your home information.
- If the hotel desk calls your room to request your credit card number and expiry date again, do not provide the information on the telephone. It could be a scam.
- Limit your use of telephone banking from a hotel room. If you must use it, be sure to change your telephone banking access code, using another landline telephone, as soon as possible afterwards.
- Do not use your computer in a hotel room to transmit sensitive personal and financial unless you know that the link is secure; for example, you are connected through virtual private network (VPN) software that requires an extra level of log-on passwords and encryption.

PROTECTING YOUR COMMUNICATIONS AND TRANSACTIONS: TELEPHONE AND FAX

3

Doing your banking over the telephone and using telephones and fax machines to make purchases and communicate with your bank representative and investment brokers are common everyday activities. Likewise, it is commonplace to receive telephone calls from telemarketers trying to sell you products or services or asking you to participate in fundraising or complete a survey. Many people carry out these everyday communications with little thought about the possibility of risk.

TELEPHONE BANKING

While having access to your accounts just a telephone call away is very convenient, telephone banking is also an electronic portal to your money. If you use telephone banking to make bill payments, transfer funds between accounts, and check your account balances, your first line of defence is to use a secure landline telephone. Online banking on the Internet is discussed in Chapter 14.

Landline Telephones

As the communications from landline (hard wire) telephones are least likely to be accessed by eavesdroppers, these telephones are the safest connections when you do telephone banking or need to discuss sensitive personal and financial information.

Cordless Telephones

The cordless or portable telephone makes it easier for someone to eavesdrop on your telephone calls. As these telephones have become more powerful and can now transmit signals over longer distances, the risk of others listening into your calls has increased. The manuals for some cordless telephones provide instructions for changing the channel if you are hearing, or getting interference, from your neighbour's cordless telephone. These instructions certainly underscore the potential lack of security.

Eavesdroppers can also obtain electronic devices to listen in on cordless telephone transmissions and capture your transactions when you are telephone banking, including the access code you enter on the keypad. Do not use a cordless telephone to do your telephone banking, except in an emergency. If you do, change your access code as soon as possible, using a regular or landline telephone.

Cellular Phones

While cordless telephones have a limited range, cell phone signals transmit much farther. It is also possible to buy devices that intercept cell phone calls including, of course, those calls made for telephone banking. Only use your cell phone for telephone banking in an emergency and then use some other more secure means to change your access code for your telephone banking as soon as possible.

PRACTICAL STEPS TO PROTECT YOURSELF
Protecting Your Telephone Banking and Personal Telephone Conversations

- Use a landline telephone for all telephone banking and for all conversations where it is important the information exchanged remains private.
- Do NOT use a cell phone for telephone banking or when you need to ensure your telephone call remains private, such as discussing private information with your health professionals, the tax authorities or your banking representative.
- Do NOT use a cell phone to change your telephone banking access code.
- If you have to use a cordless telephone or cell phone for telephone banking, change your access code as soon as possible afterwards.
- Communications on cordless phones can also be intercepted, and while the risk is less than cell phones, consider the precautions about cell phones when you use a cordless telephone.

PROTECTING YOUR ACCESS IDENTITY FOR TELEPHONE BANKING

To protect your use of telephone banking, you need to protect your telephone banking access identity (often your debit card or bankcard number) and the access code that allows you access over the telephone. Most financial institutions set rules about the nature and length of access codes, which generally are five to eight digits long and can only contain numbers and no letters.

When you set up your telephone banking, your financial services provider may assign an access code or the PIN you use for your debit card. In either case, you should immediately change this access code. Also make sure it is different from any other banking access code, PINs or passwords that you have. Note, however, that some financial systems unfortunately require that you use the same password for telephone banking and online banking on the Internet.

Low to High Risk

A thief who can access your telephone banking information can set up new bills and accounts for payment and make these payments from your account. This access is also a means to obtain information about you and your financial transactions and accounts in order to hijack your identity and carry out numerous fraudulent transactions using your name and credit worthiness.

Since telephone banking allows you to check your account from any place where you can use a telephone, one of the best defences against information theft and losses is to check your balances and transactions frequently. If you discover anomalies such as unusual transactions, you can immediately notify your financial services institution and limit your losses.

Using telephone banking when you are away from home requires additional precautions. For example, if you must use a telephone in a hotel room to do telephone banking, be sure to change your access code from a more secure landline telephone as soon as possible afterwards. This precaution is necessary because the numbers you enter into the telephone go through the private switchboard of the hotel and could be recorded. Chapter 2 discusses additional preventative steps you need to take when travelling.

PRACTICAL STEPS TO PROTECT YOURSELF
Protecting Your Telephone Banking
- Use a landline telephone and NOT a cordless or a cell phone for doing your telephone banking. If you must use a cordless or cell phone for an emergency situation, change your access code as soon as possible afterwards using a secure telephone.
- Change your access code on a regular basis. How often you change it depends on how often you use it.
- Write down your access code only if your agreement with your financial services provider permits it, and then only in a disguised manner. Keep it safely hidden.

ACCESS CODES AND PINs

While, on one hand people may complain they have too many access codes and PINs, on the other hand providers advise them to create different ones for their various debit and credit cards and for telephone and online banking and keep all of them confidential. Realistically, though, unless you use these access codes and PINs almost daily, it is an onerous task to commit each one to memory. The task is further complicated when you have access codes for other tasks, such as entering your workplace, using a home security alarm system and retrieving telephone messages at home and at work. All of these access codes should also be unique so that a loss of one number will only risk the access to one service.

Providers also consistently advise clients to select access codes and PINs that are easy to remember but hard for someone else to guess. Certainly you should not use a series of the same numbers, such as 1111, as these would be easy to guess or view over your shoulder. Similarly, you should not use any numbers that are part of your identity, such as your date of birth, driver's licence, Social Insurance Number (SIN) or other numbers that appear on your personal documents.

Creating and Disguising Your Access Codes and PINs

The agreements of some financial services and other providers stipulate that you may not write down your access code or PIN while others will allow you to write these down, provided you disguise them. Increasingly, security policies and card agreements are allowing this latter approach.

If the agreement allows you to record your PIN or access code, write it in a hidden or disguised manner that only you can decipher. Used for centuries to hide secret information, the technique is known as steganography (meaning hidden writing).

Generally, phrases are easier to remember and can be written down without being easily deciphered. An important benefit of passphrases is that they can be written in a secret code. You could then include a simple page of several phrases and obscure lists of words and numbers in your wallet, purse or address book as it would be difficult for another person to decipher your secret way of writing. And, even if someone found this list, it is unlikely that they would get it right the first time. They would need several tries, which would cancel the access.

Of note is that your financial services institution will be more likely to believe that you did not write down your PIN if the thief was not successful with the PIN on the first attempt. Success would be a clear indication that the PIN was easy to obtain or guess.

Since the keypad of many automated banking machines (ABM, also known as ATM or automated teller machine) has letters and numbers similar to a telephone keypad, you could use a passphrase for both access codes and PINs. For example, the passphrase "apples" translates to a PIN of "277537" when you enter the letters on the keypad. However, this approach will not be as easy to use where the ABM or debit machine (point-of-sale device) does not have letters printed on the keys.

Other techniques can include taking the numbers and when writing them down, increase the first number by one, the second number by two and so on. Alternatively, you could use higher numbers, and then subtract one from the first number two from the second number and so on. You could write the numbers backwards. You could also combine all of these techniques and then write the results in your address book as if the sequence is part of a telephone number.

The Resources section of this book includes tips and techniques for effectively creating strong PINs, passwords and passphrases and disguising them.

Low to High Risk

Despite the proliferation of advice and the related restrictions, many people do write their access codes and PINs down. They may write them down in places that do not seem obvious; however, thieves know the tricks and hiding places. All too frequently they find PINs and access codes in stolen wallets to use with the victim's debit card and telephone banking.

If a fraud occurs with your access code or PIN and your financial services provider determines that you had written it down, you may be found liable for the money taken from your accounts. Depending on the terms of your agreement, this liability may even extend to a situation where the unauthorized person is caught on videotape in the act of taking the money from your account.

PRACTICAL STEPS TO PROTECT YOURSELF
Protecting Your Access Codes and PINs

- Where your financial services or another provider gives you an initial PIN or access code, change it immediately to one that you have personally selected.
- Use different access codes for the various electronic banking services that you use, i.e., your access code for telephone banking, your PIN for your debit card and your password for online banking should all be different.

- Make sure your access codes and PINs are not easy for others to guess. They should NOT contain easily located numbers, such as your birth date, street address, SIN or telephone number.
- Write your access codes and PINs down only if the agreement with your financial services provider permits it, and then only in a disguised manner. Keep these safely hidden.
- Similarly, disguise any other access codes or PINs not connected with banking that you wish to write down.
- Change your access codes and PINs periodically, depending on how often you use them.
- Change your access codes and PINs immediately if you have done anything that may have compromised them.

Debit and credit cards are further discussed in Chapters 4 and 7. Chapter 8 discusses the process of authenticating your identity, for example, when you contact your provider because you have forgotten your PIN or access code. Computer and Internet passwords are discussed throughout Chapters 9 to 15.

Telephone calls

Be careful how you respond to telephone calls, particularly if the caller is a stranger. Even if you have call display, you cannot always be sure of the identity of the caller or the purpose of the call. You have likely received the typical call where you are asked to participate in a survey. Sometimes the caller's real purpose is to sell you a product or service or add your name to a mailing or telephone solicitation list that may be sold to other companies. Sometimes the caller wants information about you for fraudulent purposes.

Low to High Risk
Before responding to a telephone caller, consider the caller's identity and purpose. Fraud stories abound about people who were defrauded when a crook pretending to be a bank representative called to ask about a banking transaction or to request the person's PIN or other personal banking details. Sometimes the caller purported to be a bank inspector who needed the client's help. Banking representatives simply do not call clients to ask a customer to assist in a fraud investigation. Clearly, do NOT engage in this type of conversation. Hang up and notify the police.

PRACTICAL STEPS TO PROTECT YOURSELF
Dealing with Telephone Inquiries

- Use call display where available as it may help identify the caller. Certainly a blocked number is a clear indication that the caller does not want you to know his or her identity.
- Be wary when responding to a telephone survey. If you do decide to participate, provide very general personal and financial information, e.g., your age range rather than date of birth. Ask about the purpose of the survey and what will be done with any information you provide.
- When in doubt, confirm the identity of the caller by looking up the number in the telephone book and calling the person back.
- Do NOT provide any information about your access codes, PINs or passwords over the telephone to anyone, for any reason.
- If your financial services institution calls you to discuss an unusual transaction on your credit card, be very cautious. Ask questions to determine the person's legitimacy. Better still, look up the credit card Service Centre for your financial services institution and call the person back.
- Be very cautious about providing personal information over the telephone — the caller may be planning to defraud you.
- Always ask yourself if a request for information appears logical and reasonable and whether it is in your best interest to provide it.

FAXES

In many ways, sending and receiving faxes present similar risks as telephone calls and should be treated in much the same way. Of note is that financial services institutions and other such organizations normally will accept fax instructions to do transactions such as transferring money between accounts only when a pre-authorized arrangement is in place and on file.

Low to High Risk

A thief can easily change a fax machine to display another number on the fax and not the number of the actual machine that was used. For this reason, do not assume that a fax is from the source from which it appears to have been sent. Consider also that it is very easy to photocopy or forge letterheads and signatures. A fax that appears to be authentic could, in fact, be fraudulent.

...

Of course, if you receive a fax that you are expecting and it deals with a subject that you expected to be discussed, it would make sense to treat that fax as genuine. However, if you do not expect the fax, carefully consider whether you should respond. Similar to receiving a telephone call, you cannot be certain of the identity of the person sending the fax.

Sending a fax is comparable to sending a postcard in the physical mail. It can be read by anyone who can access the receiving fax machine. Before sending a fax with personal and financial information, consider where it is going, who may have access to it, and whether it may be stored in memory at the sending fax machine that others may access.

PRACTICAL STEPS TO PROTECT YOURSELF
Sending and Receiving Faxes

- When sending a fax, keep in mind that others may read it and not just the intended recipient.
- If you are sending personal financial or medical information, consider whether it is necessary to send this information by fax.
- Call the recipient and request that the person stand by the fax machine and collect it right away before others see it.
- Ask if the fax can be sent to a fax machine that is in a private office or other private place.
- If you have any doubts about a fax that is sent to you, confirm its authenticity. Contact the person or company that apparently has sent you the fax and ask them to confirm the message by telephone before acting on its contents.
- Unsolicited faxes that request you respond with personal information should be handled carefully. This is the equivalent of someone telephoning or e-mailing you and asking for private information that you should NOT readily provide.

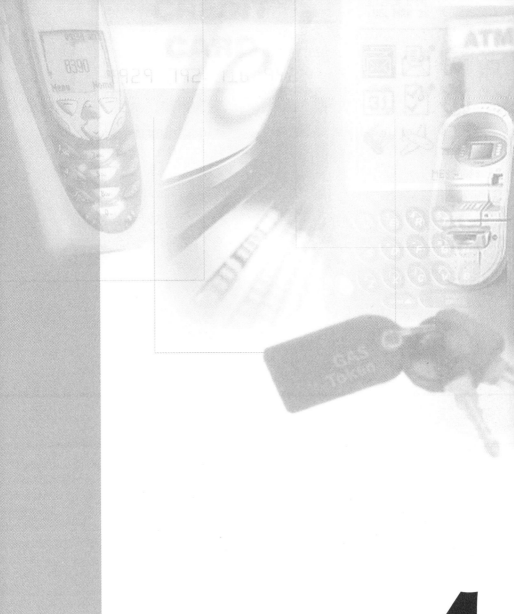

PROTECTING YOUR
DEBIT AND CREDIT CARDS 4

The swipe of a plastic card has become so commonplace for making withdrawals and purchases and doing other financial transactions that many people now carry little cash. And, many may not have given much thought to the risks associated with debit and credit cards and the payment tokens they may use at gas stations.

Generally your potential loss for credit cards is limited to a small amount, often less than $50 or even zero; whereas with your debit cards, your losses can be much higher and possibly equal the money you have in all your accounts and lines of credit with a particular financial services institution. Your losses for a payment token may be limited to your liability for the credit card to which it is linked. However, you may count on the ability to pay by credit card so much that the loss of your credit by fraud, even temporarily, can be very inconvenient, especially when travelling.

Debit cards and bankcards

The debit card issued by financial services providers (which is also called a bankcard or Interac card), along with the associated PIN, generally lets you access your accounts at automated banking machines (ABM, sometimes called ATM or automated teller machine) and make purchases at merchant point-of-sale terminals. Usually, the amount of your cash withdrawal, bill payment or purchase is immediately debited from your account. Most financial institutions set daily limits on your withdrawals and purchases.

Unlike credit cards, debit cards do NOT usually have contractual or legal limits on the amount of money you can lose if your debit card is used for fraudulent transactions. Most of the contracts that customers must sign state, in effect, that you are responsible for any withdrawals and all uses of your debit card and PIN, just as if you had signed a document for the transaction. Of course, your daily withdrawal limit provides some protection since an inability to make a withdrawal would alert you to the possibility of unauthorized transactions. But there is no liability limit on what a fraud artist might steal through purchasing goods on the debit card.

If fraudulent transactions occur with your debit card, you may be able to satisfy your financial services institution that these were not carried out by you and have your money returned. However, be aware that you may not in fact be able to get your money back. The agreement you signed to use your debit card and PIN is an authorizing document. The burden of proof is, to a large extent, on you to convince your financial institution that it was not you who used your card and PIN and that you had done nothing whatsoever to permit someone else to do so. Chapter 7 further discusses debit cards and your relationship with your financial services institution.

Limiting Debit Card Access

Be aware that your financial services provider may have automatically linked all your accounts to your debit card when it first issued your card. You should, however, have the option to select and limit the accounts and the services that are linked to your debit card. You may also be able to set up these limits for your telephone banking and online banking. Consider limiting your debit card access to just those accounts that you use for day-to-day transactions. If fewer accounts are linked, a thief who steals your debit card cannot access all your financial information and the funds in accounts to which your card is not linked (unless, of course, the thief is able to find some way of linking your other accounts to your card).

Debit Card Fraud

Some of the debit card schemes that thieves have been known to use to capture a victim's debit card number and PIN include:

- Building a fake but convincing ABM that records users' debit card numbers and PINs
- Installing a hidden camera at a point-of-sale, such as at a gas station, to record the PINs being entered
- Picking up discarded slips at ABMs, since these receipts may include debit card numbers
- Accessing a debit card number from a company's system, since many merchants store debit card numbers for each transaction
- Standing behind someone at a point-of-sale or ABM to observe the person entering a PIN (called shoulder surfing)
- Posing as a security guard or a window cleaner in a bank branch lobby and watching people enter their PINs
- Standing across the street from an ABM and using binoculars or a camcorder to record PINs, and
- Telling customers they have dropped a $20 bill and switching the debit card as it comes out from the machine when the victim bends over to retrieve the bill (commonly referred to as bait and switch).

These are not fictitious schemes; thieves have used all of these methods to cheat victims of their money.

Low to High Risk

Debit card theft is big business. A thief simply needs to know your debit card number and PIN to be able to access your money and does not necessarily need your actual debit card. Increasingly, fraudulent cards are being created, using stolen information that is then encoded in the magnetic strip on the back of the debit card. These cards may not even look authentic, as an ABM merely processes the data on the magnetic stripe and the PIN that is entered.

Regrettably, hold-ups at ABMs are becoming more commonplace. For this and other reasons, financial services institutions limit the amount of cash that can be taken out of your financial accounts in any one day. You can also choose to reduce your daily limit to protect yourself. The reduced limit will also alert you to unauthorized withdrawals if you try to make a withdrawal or bill payment and the transaction is denied.

PRACTICAL STEPS TO PROTECT YOURSELF
Protecting Your Debit Card

- Continuously safeguard your debit card and PIN; they are the keys to your financial services and accounts.
- Each time you receive a new or replacement debit card, create a new PIN at the financial services branch and sign the back of the debit card, where a signature is required.
- Limit the number of accounts linked to your debit card. Consider having debit card access to only your chequing account and NOT your savings account where you may have more money on deposit.
- Whenever possible, use a credit card rather than your debit card for shopping. This will reduce the number of merchants who have your debit card number and the number of opportunities for others to observe your PIN as you enter it.
- Each time you use your debit card, keep it in sight and make sure it is returned to you before you leave.
- Always conduct your ABM transactions when and where you feel secure. If you are uncertain about the safety of a location, do not proceed with your transactions. Go to another ABM.

- Whenever possible, use an ABM that is located in a bank branch. There have been incidents of debit cards and PINs being stolen at ABMs placed in merchant locations.
- Be cautious in shopping malls and in the lobbies of financial services institutions when the branch is closed.
- Be aware and cautious of loiterers at ABMs, even if they appear to be security guards or other workers.
- Politely ask anyone hovering near you to move back before you enter your PIN.
- When using a point-of-sale debit machine, do a visual check to ensure there is only one wire or cable connecting it.

Safeguarding Debit Card Receipts

- Do not leave your transaction slips behind; take them with you. These receipts are toxic waste and should not be discarded carelessly. Store them safely and, after you have reconciled your account, shred them before discarding.
- Reconcile your financial statements at least once a month. Contact your financial services institution immediately if you discover unexplained debit card transactions.
- If you also have telephone banking or online banking, check your account balances and activities frequently. If there are unauthorized withdrawals, take immediate action. Telephone banking is discussed in Chapter 3; online banking is discussed in Chapter 14.

If You are Held Up

- Remember your personal safety comes first. Comply with the thief's request and report the robbery to the police and to your financial services institution as soon as it is safe to do so.

CREDIT CARDS

Many people tend to be more relaxed about using their credit cards than they are about using their debit cards, as the potential for personal financial loss is often lower. The agreement with the credit card issuer usually limits your loss to a small amount, i.e., less than $50 or even zero, if the card is lost or stolen, provided you report the loss within a certain time period. The basic process is that to be liable, you, as owner of the credit card, must sign a credit card slip. In cases of dispute, the merchant must produce this slip or the amount charged to your credit card may be reversed.

In order to make all of this work, it is vital that you sign the back of the credit card and notify your financial services institution if you lose your card or notice fraudulent transactions on your account.

A Secondary Credit Card

One way that you can limit potential misuse of your credit card is to obtain a secondary credit card for which you request a much lower credit limit, e.g., $500, than you have on your primary credit card. Use this secondary credit card for transactions that may present greater risks, such as making purchases over the telephone or on the Internet, paying for food home delivery, making hotel and other travel reservations (you can use your primary credit card at check-out), using at public telephones and paying for routine and small value purchases.

If your secondary credit card is compromised, i.e., someone uses the number for fraudulent transactions, the lower limit is a deterrent. In addition, if the card is cancelled because of misuse, you will still have the use of your primary credit card.

Whether you obtain a secondary credit card from your primary credit card provider or from another financial services institution, be sure to insist on a lower credit limit than the one on your primary card. You also need to request that this limit not be automatically increased at any time.

The Extra Numbers on the Back of Your Debit and Credit Cards

Most credit cards have three or more additional digits on the back, referred to as the "card verification value". The card issuer uses these numbers to confirm your identity and possession of your credit card. As these numbers are provided for security purposes, you should only disclose them to the financial services institution. Do not disclose these numbers to other parties. Remember that the only way you can be certain that you are talking to the financial services institution is if you made the phone call.

Low to High Risk

Consider the inconvenience if someone misuses your credit card number and uses up your credit limit. While you may not have to pay for the fraudulent transactions, you will be unable to use the card for shopping or travel expenses until the problem is resolved. The credit card provider will cancel your credit card at the time that you report the problem. While the issuer deals with the fraudulent transactions, including asking you many questions, it may be some time before you receive a replacement credit card.

...

If you can also use your credit card with a PIN to withdraw cash at an ABM, your losses from your financial accounts are likely not subject to the limit in the credit card agreement. Rather than use a credit card as a debit card, request a debit card to use at ABMs. In an emergency, you could always use the credit card at a financial services institution to obtain a cash advance. By not having a credit card with a PIN number, you can limit your credit card liability for fraudulent transactions.

Generally, you can check your credit card balance and obtain the balance and sometimes the details of your recent transactions at an ABM, over the telephone, or online. You may even be able to increase your credit limit with a simple phone call to your provider.

Accessing these services usually requires your entering your credit card number but not the extra digits on the back that would at least prove that you are in possession of the card. Instead, you may be asked for the day and month of your birth, your mother's maiden name or some other fact, such as your postal code. While these questions provide some protection, keep in mind that a thief can easily obtain most of this information with minimal research. Authenticating your identity is discussed in Chapter 8.

PRACTICAL STEPS TO PROTECT YOURSELF
Protecting Your Credit Cards

- Read your credit card agreement carefully. Determine the limit of your responsibility for losses. Ask if this limit extends to cash withdrawals at an ABM and online transactions.
- Only disclose the extra three or more digit card verification value on the back of your card to the financial services institution that issued your credit card and then only when you are absolutely sure you are speaking to the issuer's representative.
- Use your credit card solely as a credit card. Use a debit card and PIN for ABM transactions.
- If you must use your credit card to withdraw cash from an ABM, guard and regularly change this PIN as you would for a debit card. Select a unique PIN for using the credit card at ABMs; do not use the same PIN that you use with any other cards.
- Obtain a secondary credit card with a low limit for use in situations where the risk exposure is higher. Ensure this limit will not be automatically increased.
- Use your primary credit card with its larger credit limit only when necessary.

- Keep your credit card receipts, reconcile them with your statement, and either store them safely or shred them before discarding. Note: Your credit card number appears on your credit card receipt.

LOST OR STOLEN CARDS

What do you do if your credit or debit card is lost, stolen, or retained by an ABM? First, make sure you know the procedures for reporting a lost or stolen card as outlined in the issuer's agreement. Notify the card issuer immediately and ask for the card to be deactivated. Keep a record of the name of the person you spoke to and the date and time that you called.

If an ABM does not return your card and the ABM is located at an open branch, you can immediately report your loss and ask for assistance. If the branch is closed or the ABM is located elsewhere, you should NOT walk away with the false impression that the card must be safe because it is in the ABM and therefore safely in the hands of your financial services institution. Follow the steps below.

PRACTICAL STEPS TO PROTECT YOURSELF
Reporting Lost or Stolen Cards
- If your debit or credit card is lost, retained by an ABM or stolen, notify the card issuer immediately and ask for the card to be deactivated.
- Make sure you have the correct telephone number for the issuer, both local and long distance. Remember, a "1-800" number will not work if you are travelling overseas.
- Keep the emergency contact numbers for your financial services institution and other card providers handy. Considering programming these numbers into your telephone for quick access. If you have a cell phone or PDA, program these numbers into it as well. Use the *Quick Contact List* discussed in Chapter 2.

Cards Retained by an ATM
- Try pressing the cancel button, as this action may release your card.
- Do not attempt to reenter your PIN, as this action will not release the card.
- Be extremely wary of any person who readily offers to help you retrieve your card. This type of "helpful" thief just happens to be there and asserts that retrying your PIN will work because "it worked for me".
- Contact your financial services institution or the card issuer immediately and ask that the card be suspended until it is back in your custody. Use a telephone number that you know is correct. Do not use a number that a stranger provides, as it could be a sting.

- Be sure to note the name of the service agent you speak to on the phone and the date and time that you instructed the financial services institution to deactivate your card.
- Although an emergency toll-free phone number may be posted at the ABM, it is useful to have the contact number readily accessible, such as programmed in your cell phone or PDA.
- Note that few debit or credit card agreements require you to notify them when an ABM retains your card. Review your agreement. Regardless, the prudent course of action is to report the loss of the card immediately and ask that it be deactivated until it is returned to you.

PAYMENT TOKENS

Payment tokens are a relatively new means of credit transactions and are currently limited to purchases at gas stations; however, it is likely that their acceptance and usage will spread. A payment token is a small device that can be attached to a key chain that is used to pay for gas purchases by simply holding the token at a specific spot on the service station's gas pump.

Some payment tokens have a contact telephone number printed on the token itself; however, this is of little help if the token is lost or stolen. Be sure to record this information, along with the serial number, on your *Quick Contact List* discussed in Chapter 2.

Low to Moderate Risk

When applying for the payment token, you will be asked to provide your credit card number and, if applicable, your frequent user points card number. The issuer usually keeps this information in its central database of customers. The computer memory chip inside the payment token is linked to your credit card number and frequent user points account and connects to complete the transaction.

As you do not need to sign for the purchase or enter a PIN or access code, your payment token can be used by anyone. Treat it the same way you would cash.

PRACTICAL STEPS TO PROTECT YOURSELF

Protecting Your Payment Tokens

- Do not lend your payment token to others. Treat it like cash.
- Safeguard your payment token as you would your debit and credit cards. If it is lost or stolen, immediately contact the company that issued it and the credit card issuer to which the token is linked.
- Keep a record of the contact number and the serial number of the token so you can immediately deactivate it if it is lost or stolen. Use the *Quick Contact List* discussed in Chapter 2.
- Ask the payment token issuer and your financial services credit card issuer what is your liability if the token is lost or stolen.

PROTECTING AND DISPOSING OF SENSITIVE DOCUMENTS

5

Where do you store your most sensitive information, such as your social insurance card, bankbooks, cheques and tax records? How do you dispose of receipts, correspondence and records that you no longer need?

SAFEKEEPING OF IMPORTANT DOCUMENTS

Documents that include sensitive personal information, such as SIN cards, passports, and birth certificates, need to be kept in a safe place. These documents should NOT be routinely carried on your person but should be readily accessible if you need them. You should also safeguard credit cards that you use only occasionally and financial information, such as spare chequebooks, old income tax returns, financial and credit card statements and records, and credit bureau reports. Back-up disks and CD-ROMs of computerized information and financial records should also be stored in a safe place, as discussed in Chapter 10.

Safety Deposit Box

A safety deposit box is one way to protect valuable jewelry, family heirlooms and important documents, but it is only an effective safeguard if you use it regularly. Too often the distance and limited access hours will mean some important items are left at home until the next visit to the safety deposit box or they never get there at all.

Locked Storage Box

As many bank branches no longer provide safety deposit boxes, you may be using a fireproof, locked storage box at home to store your important documents and valuables. While this is an economical way to store passports, SIN cards and other important documents, the box must be secured, such as bolted to a permanent fixture, to prevent a thief from taking the box and its contents.

Home Safe

Increasingly, many people now invest in a home safe to protect their personal information and other valuables in their homes. A home safe is convenient as you have easy access to these items when you need them. As the prices, types and sizes of home safes vary, you need to determine what documents and articles you want need to store in the safe before purchasing one. You should also consider the specific risks you need to minimize, including theft, disclosure, fire and smoke and water damage. These factors will help you determine the type and size of safe that will best meet your needs.

Some home safes are simple lock boxes that can be bolted to a permanent fixture to prevent theft. These are relatively inexpensive and offer adequate security for basic items. As some are fire and heat resistant and others are fire and/or water proof, you should know what the rating means and the protection afforded in the event of a major fire. Simply put, if you plan to store important, irretrievable documents and computerized information, you will want to ensure that the contents of the safe are protected if a major fire or flood occurs.

At the high end is the stand-up safe that weighs many hundreds of pounds and requires a moving crew to deliver and place it. While this type of home safe is expensive, many people find peace of mind knowing that all their personal information and items are well protected from theft, disclosure and fire and water damage, yet are easily accessible when necessary.

PRACTICAL STEPS TO PROTECT YOURSELF
Safeguarding Your Documents and Valuables
- Keep a record of the contents of your safety deposit box, locked storage box or home safe.
- If you are using a locked storage box or small safe to store important documents in your home, bolt it to a permanent fixture to ensure it is not easily removed.

SAFE DISPOSAL
Check the contents of your wastebasket and garbage pail. You may find that you have discarded documents without giving much thought to the information they provide about your money, privacy and identity. Your garbage may include junk mail or magazines that include your name and address on a mailing label, an expired credit card or driver's licence, an old utility bill, a computer disk with files still on it or even old tax returns. These sources of information need to be carefully destroyed before being discarded so that no one can reconstruct them to find out personal information about you.

"Toxic Waste" Documents

"Toxic waste" includes any document with your name and address and other personal and financial information. Toxic waste should never be tossed intact into a recycling box or garbage bag for the next collection. Safe disposal may take some care and organization, but the effort could save you a great deal of time and anxiety if your identity was hijacked.

Small quantities of paper are relatively easy to destroy, such as mailing labels, purchase slips from stores with your account numbers and signature, and transaction slips from ABMs. Larger documents such as old files take more work and effort to destroy safely.

Paper Shredder

If you have a lot of toxic waste, consider purchasing a home paper shredder for disposing of paper documents. Choose a shredder that will shred multiple pages at a time and cuts finely (less than one quarter of an inch). The effectiveness of the shredder depends on the quality and size of the cutting blades. A shredder that cuts very fine strips makes it extremely difficult for someone to reconstruct the shredded content. Crosscutting shredders are the most expensive models and make it virtually impossible to reconstruct the original page of information.

Fire

If you have a fireplace, wood-burning stove or outside fire receptacle, burn your discarded paper documents. Make sure they are completely destroyed before extinguishing or leaving the fire.

Scissors

Cut up plastic cards before throwing them out. First scratch out your signature and then cross cut horizontally through the card number and any magnetic stripe on the back. As an extra precaution, discard the cut-up pieces in several garbage bags or bins and even over several garbage collections to eliminate the chance that someone will find all the pieces and reconstruct or reuse the information.

Blender

Use a blender to dispose of small quantities of paper. Put small pieces of paper in the blender along with some water and pulverize them. The pulp can then be added to your compost. Paper documents disposed of in this way are impossible to reconstruct.

High Risk

Thieves who are intent on finding information about you and invading your privacy will sort through your household and office garbage to find the information they need. Commonly known as "dumpster divers", these thieves are a particular threat at apartment buildings or condominiums where the dumpster contains a wealth of information about many people.

PRACTICAL STEPS TO PROTECT YOURSELF
Disposing of Toxic Documents and Cards

- **Tear it up:** Small quantities of paper and credit and debit card slips can simply be torn up by hand.
- **Burn it:** Paper can easily be discarded in a wood-burning fireplace, stove or cottage bonfire.
- **Shred it:** A paper shredder is a simple way to dispose of quantities of paper. Buy the best model you can afford.
- **Cut it up:** Use scissors to cut up expired plastic debit and credit cards, expired driver's licences and any other laminated documents. Be sure to scratch the magnetic strip first.
- **Process in the blender:** Tear up paper, add some water and process it in a kitchen blender.

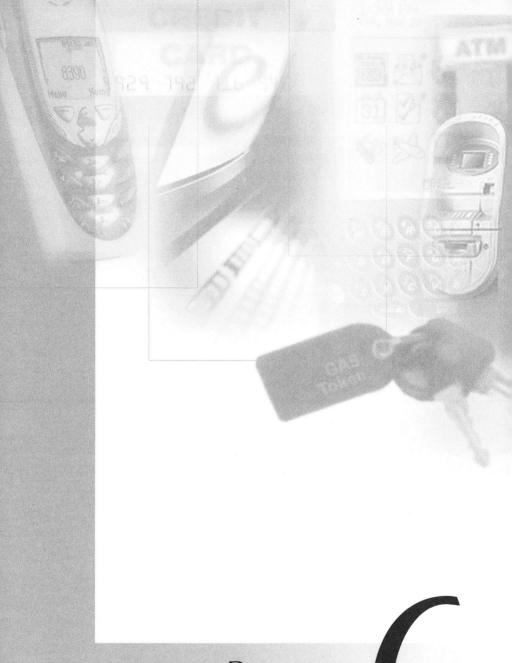

DEALING WITH REQUESTS FOR INFORMATION: GOVERNMENT AGENCIES AND OTHER ORGANIZATIONS

6

How do you respond when sales clerks ask you to provide your name, address and telephone number when ringing up a purchase? Have you been asked to provide your social insurance number as identification? When asked to provide personal information, do you know when the request is a legal requirement and when you can decline providing certain information?

This chapter discusses the many information relationships you may have with the government and various organizations. The following chapter discusses your information relationships with your financial services institution.

LEGISLATED INFORMATION DISCLOSURE

Various government departments and agencies have legislated rights to collect certain personal information about you. Strict regulation and legislation includes provisions for the sharing of this information with other departments and, at times, with third parties.

For example, various levels of government can request personal information for processing:
- Income tax returns
- Driver's licence applications
- Passport applications
- Property taxes
- Social Insurance Numbers (SIN)
- Birth certificates
- Marriage licences, and
- Government health programs (e.g., OHIP in Ontario).

In addition, your employer may request certain personal information in order to meet its reporting requirements. When you open a financial account, obtain a credit card, apply for a loan or purchase an insurance policy, the provider may request certain information as discussed later in this chapter. The information relationship you have with your financial services institution is discussed in Chapter 7.

Your Information Relationship with Government Agencies

It is important to be aware as to when your information must be provided and when it is optional. If you are asked to provide personal information that is not required by law, inquire as to the necessity and purpose. Consider whether it is in your best interest to provide it.

A government agency may also provide third parties with access to certain information on a fee-for-service basis. In Ontario, for example, insurance companies can access an Ontario resident's driver's licence details and driving record.

A driver's licence is a good example of how a small amount of information provided on an application can have other information added to it. The provincial driving record referenced to your driver's licence number may include:
- Traffic offences, including those occurring in another jurisdiction that has information exchange agreements with the jurisdiction that issued your driver's licence
- Unpaid parking fines that you must pay prior to renewing your licence
- The record of the emission control inspection of your car, and
- If your driver's license has been suspended, information about the proceeding or medical condition that led to the suspension.

Requesting Copies of Your Data

Legislation provides that you may request a copy of data that a government department has on file about you and also sets out defined processes for correcting any inaccurate or incomplete data. If you have questions about your privacy or cannot satisfactorily resolve a problem, contact the Office of the Privacy Commissioner of the applicable federal or provincial government.

Low Risk

Overall, the various levels of government:
- Gather data on individuals as permitted by law and regulation
- Share data with other departments and governments where law so permits
- Share data with third parties where there is an obvious need to do so and where law or regulation permits this sharing
- Usually set minimum standards that all departments must follow to protect the accuracy and privacy of the individual's personal data, and
- Provide a privacy office or commissioner to protect the individual's privacy and provide help with privacy issues.

...

There are strict laws as to who is entitled to see information concerning an individual that the government maintains. There are also quality assurance procedures that set out the minimum control processes that each federal or provincial/territorial government department must put in place to help ensure the privacy and accuracy of data concerning you.

PRACTICAL STEPS TO PROTECT YOURSELF
Providing Personal Information to the Government

- Send income tax returns and other important documents and applications to the government by registered mail or through secured government online services.
- Consider going to government offices in person to renew documents, such as a driver's licence or a passport. Arrange to pick these up when they are ready rather than having them mailed to you.
- Ask for a copy of your information file and review it to ensure the information is complete and accurate, particularly if others may be referring to it in the near future.

YOUR SOCIAL INSURANCE NUMBER

Your social insurance number (SIN) is a unique identifier. While many people tend to provide their SIN or show their card on request, this information should not be freely provided to anyone who asks for it, as it is very useful for those who want to invade your privacy or steal your data.

Organizations within and outside the government ask for the SIN because it is a simple means of identification. A company may request a SIN number to ensure it does not confuse a customer with someone who has a similar name. Some companies may even inappropriately build the SIN into the customer's account number.

Although only certain government departments and programs are authorized to collect and use the SIN, **no legislation prohibits organizations from asking for it**. To protect this confidential information, you should know when it is appropriate to provide your SIN and when it is optional.

Disclosing Your SIN

The number of occasions when you are legally required to provide your SIN is actually very limited. Generally, the use of your SIN is restricted to income-related information, such as:

- Financial services institutions are required by law to ask you to provide it for income-generating deposits.
- A select and limited number of federal government departments and programs are specifically authorized to collect the SIN.
- The Canada Customs and Revenue Agency (CCRA) uses the SIN for tax reporting purposes.

Some other legislated uses of the SIN (and legislation that regulates its use) include:

- Canadian Pension Plan, Old Age Security and Employment Insurance contributions or claims (the original purposes for establishing the SIN)
- Income tax identification, and
- Banks, trust companies, caisse populaires and stockbrokers when they sell you financial products (GICs or Canada Savings Bonds) or services (bank accounts) that generate interest, as they must declare your interest income to the CCRA.

There are many other examples where legislation allows government departments or programs to request your SIN card. To obtain more information about privacy and your SIN, contact:

> The Office of the Privacy Commissioner of Canada
> 112 Kent Street
> Ottawa, ON
> K1A 1H3
> Toll-free telephone: 1-800-282-1376

Or, visit these federal government websites:

> www.privcom.gc.ca
> www.hrdc-drhc.gc.ca/sin/

High Risk

Your SIN is very useful information if someone wants to hijack your identity. It should NOT be used as personal identification in a general sense. If you are not legally required to provide your SIN (and you are not satisfied with the explanation), do not disclose it. Offer other proof of your identification. If you are refused a product or service because you will not provide your SIN, register a complaint with the Privacy Commission of Canada or your province or territory.

PRACTICAL STEPS TO PROTECT YOURSELF
Disclosing Your SIN
- Ask if you are required by law to provide your SIN.
- Do NOT disclose your SIN if it is not legally required.

INSURANCE COMPANIES

When you apply for insurance, such as household, term or whole life, income protection or automobile insurance, the insurance company will request a great deal of information about you. The companies, of course, also keep records of each insured's claims in order to set premium rates. If an insured has too many claims, the insurer may cancel the policy. Health insurers also retain a great deal of information about you and your claims.

Generally, insurance policies are contracts of "utmost good faith", meaning that the insurance company has the right to make the assumption that you have answered all questions completely and honestly and have disclosed to them all circumstances that would be relevant to the issuing of a policy and keeping it in force. If there are errors or omissions on the insurance application, the insurer may find the policy invalid when you make a claim. Generally, you are obliged to tell the insurance company about changes in your circumstances to update the answers you provided on the original application.

Low to Moderate Risk

You cannot examine the procedures the insurance company uses to ensure the details in their electronic files are correctly entered from the form you have filled out. Your best protection is to keep copies of forms and questionnaires you have completed and store these in a safe place. If the insurer's computer records are wrong, these copies will help you to substantiate the information that you originally provided. This also applies to any changes in your information that you provide. Provide these changes in writing and keep a copy.

PRACTICAL STEPS TO PROTECT YOURSELF
Monitoring Your Insurance Records
- Keep copies of all information provided to an insurance company. If you dispute a claim, these copies will be helpful in substantiating the information you provided.

- Ask about the insurance company's policies and processes for sharing your information with other organizations. Only an agent or broker should be able to access this information. Think carefully if you get a different answer.
- Ask about the procedure for notifying the insurance company of changes to your information or circumstances.
- Request a copy of the information the insurance company has on file about you and check it for completeness and accuracy.

PROFESSIONAL SERVICE PROVIDERS

Almost all professional service providers you work with have private and confidential information about you. Your lawyer may have a copy of your will, details concerning your mortgage and many more pieces of confidential information; your chartered accountant may have information about your finances and investments and copies of tax returns he or she has prepared for you. Of course, professionals are subject to the rules of professional conduct for their profession and must treat all client information as private and confidential within the bounds of any exceptions that may be imposed by law.

As everyone sees health care providers, they are discussed below as an illustration of how to deal with professionals who have confidential information about you, as the approach is much the same for all professional services. Your dentist, doctor, massage therapist and other healthcare providers maintain private records with your personal health information, such as health questionnaires, test results, diagnoses, treatments and prescriptions.

Healthcare providers are required to share some of this information with private health plans and government health programs. Doctors are also legally bound to report certain diseases and health conditions to the government or public health. For example, a doctor must report any condition to the government that would prohibit a patient from driving.

Low Risk

Your consent is required when a professional shares or requests information about you. The exception would be in the case of a medical or other emergency. If the professional is required by law to provide information to the government or an agency, you should be informed about this. You may be asked to sign a consent form to authorize the professional to disclose or access your information.

OTHER ORGANIZATIONS

The proliferation of large information systems and the need for organizations to know their customers mean that various companies often ask you to provide personal information. The information you provide in writing or input on a form is usually entered into a computer database and available to a large number of employees in that department or agency. It may even be provided to third parties.

Companies routinely maintain databases of customer information so that they can use this data for strategic planning, as well as marketing products and services by mail, e-mail, telephone or fax, based on your preferences, buying patterns and sometimes simply your postal code.

The Personal Information Protection and Electronic Documents Act

In Canada, privacy and the use of electronic information are now subject to an Act of Parliament, the *Personal Information Protection and Electronic Documents Act 2000* (PIPEDA). Enterprises are required to comply with principles that are intended to protect the consumer. Privacy issues are further discussed in Chapter 13.

Low to Moderate Risk

A person who is reluctant to share personal information certainly has the right to not apply for an insurance policy, to forego participating in certain activities, or to refrain from making certain applications. This approach would be a bit extreme and perhaps very inconvenient. However, you do NOT have to provide personal information when you purchase items such as batteries or toothpaste. You have a choice.

You can also choose the organization with which you will do business and ask questions to determine the steps it takes to protect your privacy. You do not need detailed technical explanations about an organization's systems security nor should you expect the organization to provide particulars of its privacy systems, processes and controls. However, you should ask questions to gain assurance that the organization is doing its part to protect your privacy and that the information they are requesting is in YOUR best interest.

...

When you are asked to provide personal information, ask:
- Why is this information required?
- How will it be used?
- Who will have access to it?
- How long will it be kept?
- How will it be destroyed?
- Will it be shared with others?

If you are not satisfied with the answers, do not provide the information. If you are denied service because you do not wish to provide certain information, complain to the management of that organization. If your dispute is with government, complain to the Office of the Privacy Commissioner of Canada or the Privacy Commissioner in your province or territory.

For more information and helpful resources, visit the website of The Privacy Commissioner of Canada at http://www.privcom.gc.ca

PRACTICAL STEPS TO PROTECT YOURSELF
Responding to an Organization's Request for Personal Information
- When asked to provide personal information, ask if disclosure is a legal requirement.
- If you are NOT required to provide the information by law, ask why it is required, who can access it, and whether it will be shared.
- If a telemarketer asks you to participate in a telephone survey, the person could be collecting the information for marketing purposes. As you do not know the identity of the person calling, it is risky to respond. Consider that the person may actually be collecting this information for fraudulent purposes.

CREDIT BUREAUS
In Canada, there are two credit bureaus — Equifax Canada Inc. and TransUnion Canada, both of which are privately owned. You cannot prevent these credit bureaus from maintaining records about your credit and credit history. Many organizations, such as your financial services institution, routinely file reports about an individual's credit with these credit bureaus. Other organizations, such as stores and other creditors, will report to them only when problems arise, such as late or overdue payments or a failure to settle an account. If your account has been sent for collection to a credit agency, this information will appear on your credit report.

Your credit history includes information and your personal history, such as:
- Your credit card accounts (i.e., bank, store, gas credit cards), credit limit and your payment history
- Your personal lines of credit
- Your loans and the payment records, and
- Your lease payments for vehicles and other leased assets.

The file includes the dates on which you opened the account or received a loan and when you repaid it. Payment history and loan repayments generally include the value of payments that were more than a certain number of days late, for example, over 30, 60 or 90 days late, depending on the terms. As these records are categorized, they do not necessarily show the full details of the payments.

Certain credit information is not reported and retained, for example, mortgages, property taxes, income taxes, utility bills and records of out-of-country lines of credit and credit cards. While property and income taxes and utility bills are not viewed as credit, any payment delinquency or a non-payment judgment made against you for any reason will likely be reported and included in your credit history.

The credit bureaus maintain your credit history; however, they do not have information about your financial accounts or investments. This credit information is the same information that would be provided to anyone authorized to check your record, if, for example, you applied for a new loan or credit card. For this reason, it is important that you know what is on file, as erroneous data would affect your credit rating.

How to Check Your Credit Report

Consider reviewing your credit record at least once a year to ensure the information is accurate and current. You have a right to correct any wrong or out-of-date information. Your credit report will also provide information about anyone who has recently inquired about your credit record. If you did not authorize the inquiry, ask for an explanation.

Obtaining a copy of your credit report is a straightforward process. Of course, you will be asked to provide information to authenticate your identity — your name, date of birth, addresses in the last three to five years, and your signature as well as two other pieces of proof of your identity. For these additional proofs of identity, you may be asked to provide copies of recent utility bills in your name, your passport, driver's licence, birth certificate or citizenship card, or a T-4 slip. These authentication checks are intended to ensure that no one else accesses your most sensitive personal and financial information.

To contact the credit bureaus, look in the white pages of your telephone book or go to their websites:

Equifax Canada	www.equifax.com
TransUnion Canada	www.tuc.ca

The websites provide instructions on how to obtain a copy of your credit report, the company's privacy policy, and the nature of the information it retains about you. If you do not want to wait for the report to arrive in the mail, you may be able to access it through the website once your identity is properly authenticated and you have paid the requisite fee. Other members of your family who are involved in applying for any loan may wish to do the same.

Low to High Risk

Your personal credit record is very important information, as erroneous data would affect your credit rating. You have a right to ensure that your record is correct and that it is managed in your best interest.

If you believe that your identity is under attack, promptly notify both credit bureaus and discuss your concerns. They will note your concerns on your credit report to help prevent the thief from applying and obtaining credit in your name. Chapter 16 further discusses what to do if you suspect you are a victim of identity theft.

PRACTICAL STEPS TO PROTECT YOURSELF
Monitoring Your Credit Report

- Before you apply for a loan, mortgage or increased limit on your credit card or other credit, obtain a copy of your credit report to ensure its accuracy.
- If you have several outstanding credit or repayment issues, including personal lines of credit and loans, obtain and review your credit report at least once a year.
- Be wary of companies that claim to repair bad credit. Some companies are scams that charge steep fees and do not improve the client's credit rating in any way.

DEALING WITH
REQUESTS FOR INFORMATION:
FINANCIAL SERVICES INSTITUTIONS

7

Financial services institutions gather a wealth of information about their clients. In part, they must abide by what is known as the "know your client rules"; that is by law and the rules of their industry association, they must request certain information from their clients. This information is required so that they offer products and services that meet individuals' financial needs and situation as well as their tolerance for financial risk. These are valid requests for information as they help the financial services institution better serve its clients. When you open an account, they must also confirm your identity and the sources of your deposits to protect against money laundering.

YOUR INFORMATION RELATIONSHIP WITH YOUR FINANCIAL SERVICES INSTITUTION

Providing certain personal information to a financial services institution is mandatory when you want to open an account or do other financial business. You may be asked to provide additional information and you have a choice as to whether you will provide this information. Keep in mind that the more information you provide, the more likely you will receive marketing telephone calls, e-mail, faxes and mail about the provider's other services or products.

Your financial services institution maintains a CIF (customer information file) that contains records of matters such as your credit card transactions, loans and mortgages, payment history, and the volume and pattern of deposits and withdrawals on your accounts. Each time you contact a representative about matters, such as questioning charges on your credit card or unexplained withdrawals on your accounts, your CIF is accessed as an information source.

In this increasingly anonymous electronic age, many people do their deposits, withdrawals and bill payments electronically and may never go into a branch. However, it is advantageous to have a personal relationship with a financial services officer because it is important to have someone there who knows you as a person, has reason to trust you, and will advocate on your behalf to resolve any problems you may have. As some financial services institutions now use call centres for first response customer service, ask your financial services representative or officer for a direct telephone number at the branch.

Your financial transactions

Financial services institutions do not review all items charged to your bank accounts and credit cards. Millions of items are processed electronically without an employee making an item-by-item review of the transactions. For this reason, it is very important that you check your account and credit card statements to ensure all items are valid and correct and all deposits, withdrawals and payments have been correctly credited and debited.

Low to High Risk

The agreement you signed when you opened your account usually gives you a limited amount of time in which you can challenge any errors or omissions on your account. This period is typically 30 days. With online and telephone banking services, you can easily monitor your accounts and the transactions regularly in addition to reviewing statements received in the mail.

Similarly, check your credit card balances periodically and not just when statements arrive. Under the terms of your agreement, you are responsible for questioning transactions within a limited time period, typically within 30 days of receiving your statement. If you do not act during that time period, you may find yourself responsible for fraudulent transactions that have been processed or at least be in dispute with your financial services institution.

PRACTICAL STEPS TO PROTECT YOURSELF
Monitoring Your Financial Accounts

- Establish and maintain a long-term, positive relationship with your financial services institution. Get to know a financial services officer or broker so that you will have an advocate if you experience problems.
- When you provide personal information or fill out a form, ask if the information is mandatory.
- For information that is optional, ask why the information is being requested and if its purpose is not in your best interest, do not provide it.
- Check your bank accounts, credit card records and brokerage accounts regularly and act swiftly if you believe transactions are missing, incorrect or fraudulent.
- Consider picking up new cheques, debit and credit cards and statements at the branch rather than having these sent to you in the mail.

DEBIT AND CREDIT CARDS

Debit cards and credit cards require special attention, as the incidents of card fraud are rising. Your debit and credit card agreements set out your liability and responsibilities. Make sure you understand the provisions of these agreements and your obligations before a problem arises. In particular, you should know the process if someone makes fraudulent withdrawals or purchases using your debit or credit card. Debit and credit cards are further discussed in Chapter 4.

Debit Cards

The typical debit card agreement sets out that you are legally responsible for all transactions made with your debit card and PIN (including telephone banking and online banking if you use these services). In effect, the agreement usually states that the use of your debit card together with your PIN is the same transaction as if you had signed a cheque, deposit, or withdrawal slip. The amount of your loss could exceed your account balance if you have overdraft protection or a line of credit linked to the account. The financial services institution typically reserves the right to change the agreement at any time and notify you of these changes in a manner of their choosing, such as posting a notice in the branch.

The agreement also sets out how the provider will deal with fraudulent transactions. Note the wording of the provisions under which your explanations may be accepted or rejected. Depending on the agreement, you may be liable for losses if it is established that you had written down your PIN or given your card (along with the PIN) to someone else, including a family member, to withdraw money or to make purchases. The agreement may provide that you may not be liable for unauthorized transactions if they are due to circumstances beyond your control; that is, you did not knowingly contribute to the false transactions and the situation was beyond your control. Usually it sets out that you are not responsible once you have reported the loss of your debit card to the financial services institution or reported that the debit card number has been used to make transactions you did NOT initiate.

To make informed choices, make sure you understand the provisions of your most recent (and possibly amended) agreement, the procedure for notifying you of any changes to this contract, and the process for resolving a dispute.

The Process for Resolving Debit Card Disputes

The Canadian Code of Practice for Consumer Debit Card Services is a voluntary code of practice developed in consultation with consumer organizations, financial services institutions, retailers and federal and provincial governments. Strategis (the Canadian government's business and consumer website) at http://www.strategis.gc.ca provides more information about this Code.

The Code includes a requirement that consumers be given a description of the process a financial services institution uses to resolve disputes. It is prudent to review this with your financial services institution before any disputes might arise.

If you have a debit card dispute, the four-step process is:
- First contact your financial services branch or servicing centre.
- If you are not satisfied with the provider's action or explanation, speak to a regional, area or business line manager.
- If you are dissatisfied with the way the dispute is handled or the nature of the financial service provided, contact your financial services provider's ombudsman.
- If you are still dissatisfied with the handling of the matter, take your complaint to the Canadian Banking Ombudsman, which is an independent body appointed by the federal government to provide impartial and prompt resolution of service complaints.

All financial service institutions should provide pamphlets or brochures or other sources of information explaining this complaint and escalation process.

You can contact the Canadian Banking Ombudsman at:

> Ombudsman for Banking Services and Investments
> 4950 Yonge Street, Suite #1602
> North York, Ontario
> M2N 6K1
> Telephone: 1-888-451-4519 or 416-287-2877
> Fax: 1-888-422-2865 or 416-225-4722
> www.obsi.ca

Moderate to High Risk

Debit cards present inherently higher risks than credit cards. Debit card slips printed out by merchants often contain your card number. Consider also that someone may observe you entering your PIN. If you use the same debit card number and PIN for accessing telephone and/or online banking, your financial accounts are at greater risk.

If you are a victim of debit card fraud, the agreement you have signed with your financial services provider may, in fact, put the onus of proof on you. You may have to convince the provider of your innocence in order to recover your money. In contrast, credit cards usually have a small limitation of liability for fraudulent transactions, provided you have reported the loss or problem within a given time period, and the burden of proof is placed on the merchant or organization to produce your signature as authorization.

PRACTICAL STEPS TO PROTECT YOURSELF
Protecting Your Debit Card Relationship

- Read your debit card agreement carefully. Ask how you will be notified of changes to the agreement.
- Ask if the same PIN must be used for both your debit card and telephone or online banking. To reduce your risk, your debit card PIN should NOT be the same as the access codes you use for telephone banking and online banking.
- Determine if your PIN can be longer than 4 digits (the longer the better).
- Know where and how you can change your PIN.
- Ask if the ABM prints a list of recent transactions to help you monitor your financial accounts.
- Determine which financial accounts are linked to your debit card and consider linking only one of your accounts rather than several.
- Have contact information readily available for reporting fraudulent transactions made with your debit card. The provider should immediately cancel the access when you report a problem.
- Know the dispute process if fraudulent transactions are made using your debit card.

Credit Cards

If you are going to attach a PIN to your credit card so that you can use it as a debit card, the previous discussion about debit cards and the related risks apply. However, as discussed in Chapter 4, the best practice is to use your credit card solely as a credit card and not for accessing your financial accounts.

Low to High Risk

The preventative steps for minimizing your risks are similar for credit and debit cards. If you use your credit card solely as a credit card, your liability for fraudulent transactions may be minimal, e.g., $50 or less depending on the agreement. Unlike debit cards, the burden of proof is placed on the merchant or organization to produce your signature as authorization. Remember, you do have a responsibility to notify the financial services institution as soon as you suspect a problem.

As discussed in Chapter 4, it is good practice to limit your risk by using a secondary credit card with a small credit line for routine purchases and purchases on the Internet or by telephone. It also ensures that in the event of a fraud on your secondary card, your principal credit card will not be compromised and your credit will be available to you.

PRACTICAL STEPS TO PROTECT YOURSELF
Protecting Your Credit Card Relationship
- Read your credit card agreement carefully, particularly the provision for your maximum liability for fraudulent transactions.
- Find out how the provider will notify you of changes to this agreement.
- Have contact information readily available for reporting a lost or stolen credit card or suspicious transactions. The provider should immediately cancel your card when you report a problem. Find out how long it takes to issue a replacement card and if you can get a replacement card if the loss occurs while you are travelling.
- Ask the provider how disputes are resolved, particularly if fraudulent transactions are made with your credit card.
- Find out if you can monitor your credit card balance and transactions online or by telephone.
- Enquire about the process for authenticating your identity when you contact the credit card provider by telephone or online. Authentication is discussed in Chapter 8.

Reducing Your Credit Card Risk
- Do NOT use your credit card as a debit card. If you do use a credit card with a PIN for cash withdrawals, change the PIN frequently.
- Use your secondary credit card with the low limit for higher risk activities, such as purchases over the telephone and making hotel reservations.

- Use your credit card when you go shopping; the less you use your debit card the less likely it will be compromised. Use your primary card for major purchases to safeguard the availability of this larger credit line.

TELEPHONE BANKING

As discussed in Chapter 3, telephone banking is an attractive financial service that allows you to transfer money between your accounts, make payments and transfer money from a line of credit into one of your financial accounts. This latter ability may be completely electronic or may require that you speak to a financial services officer.

You may have to sign an additional agreement for telephone banking. If the provider has asked you to sign a separate agreement for this service, read it carefully, even if you are already using telephone banking.

Online financial services are discussed in Chapter 14.

Low to High Risk

You may have access to telephone banking and not know it. Some financial services institutions automatically set up your debit card number for telephone banking at the time they issue the debit card. If this is the case and you plan to use telephone banking, change the access code. Do NOT use the same PIN for your debit card and your telephone banking access code.

If you do not want access to telephone banking, ask your financial services institution if you have the option to decline having this service linked to your debit card.

PRACTICAL STEPS TO PROTECT YOURSELF
Protecting Your Telephone Banking Relationship

- Ask if telephone banking is automatically linked to your debit card. If yes, ask if you can decline this service if you do not intend to ever use it.
- Ask if you can select an access code for telephone banking that is unique and separate from your other PINs and passwords.
- Enquire about the process for authenticating your identity when you contact the provider in person or through the telephone banking system. Authentication is discussed in Chapter 8.

- Find out how the provider will notify you of changes to your telephone banking agreement.
- Have contact information readily available for reporting fraudulent transactions made with your telephone banking access. The provider should immediately cancel the access when you report a problem.
- Read the agreement carefully, particularly the dispute resolution process if you discover fraudulent transactions in your accounts.

AUTHENTICATING YOUR IDENTITY

8

Organizations "authenticate" their customers through numerous inter-actions every day. Today as there is less face-to-face recognition by which to authenticate identity, it may be verified with requests for personal information, such as your date of birth, address or SIN or with electronic identifiers, such as your debit card and PIN.

Authenticating your identity is about what you can, and should, expect of others when they verify your identity, such that the process is easy and convenient for you, yet very difficult for an impostor. Two important issues you need to know are:

- The information about you is current and valid, including such things as your most recent transactions, and
- The organization performs a sufficient degree of checking and due diligence to satisfy itself that it is actually you who is contacting it or doing the transaction.

There is, however, a delicate balance between an organization knowing enough about you in order to authenticate your identity and an organization having personal information that intrudes on your privacy.

AUTHENTICATION CONTROLS

The organization or person authenticating you wants to do it quickly and effectively so as not to inconvenience you. They must also do it reliably because if they get a false authentication when it really is you, neither you nor the organization is going to be satisfied or happy. At the same time, you want to feel that the authentication of you is effective and stringent enough that someone else could not easily pass the authentication "test" to invade your money, privacy and identity.

For example, if you have enrolled for telephone banking, your financial services provider knows who you are. Each time you use the service, it will verify your identity, typically through your use of your bankcard number and an access code. If you forget your access code, you can telephone your financial services provider and ask for a new one. This process is a test of the effectiveness and strength of its authentication process. If you are simply asked questions regarding your bankcard number, address or postal code, your date of birth, and your chequing account number, you should be very concerned. Someone else, particularly someone who knows you, could easily obtain all this information.

To further protect customers, financial services institutions and other organizations are increasingly asking customers to provide a "shared secret" or an additional "pass code". This may be the answer to a simple question that you have agreed upon: "What is the colour of your car?" or "What is the name of your dog?" If the question is too simple, an identity thief may already know, or could easily find, this information. Other techniques include the CCRA asking you to state the amount on line 150 of your last year's tax assessment notice.

As organizations know your home telephone number, the identi-call telephone feature may be used to check that your call is coming from your home. This helps authenticate that it is you making the call.

Your Mother's Maiden Name

You may have been asked to provide your mother's maiden name as a way of authenticating your identity when making a telephone inquiry. This information is frequently a security requirement when you call to request information, as your response helps to authenticate your identity.

In the past, the mother's maiden name was a useful piece of information for confirming a caller's identity. In today's electronically connected world, however, a thief intent on using your debit and credit cards or hijacking your identity can readily determine your mother's maiden name. One of the simplest places to look is on the many family websites posted on the Internet that show the family's genealogy and, of course, maiden names and much more. In addition, since women today often retain their maiden names after marriage, or revert to it after divorce, the maiden name is readily available for anyone who wants this information.

Of course, you must provide your mother's maiden name when completing an application for a passport or similar document. For all other requests, ask why the information is being collected and whether it will be verified. Where the provision of your mother's maiden name is not a legal requirement, consider using a creative adaptation of the name to make this identifier a viable security check that another person cannot replicate; for example:
• Use your mother's middle name.
• Spell your mother's maiden name differently.

- Add a phrase to the name. For example, "Gaisten" could be used for Gaston or "Wingfield" for Wing.
- Or, provide another name altogether.

Be sure to select a version or alternate name that you will remember. You could also point out that use of the mother's maiden name for identification is out of date and offer an alternative question and shared answer as a means of authenticating your identity.

Low to High Risk

As the issues surrounding authentication are difficult to solve, it is not an easy risk to manage. Like many people, you may have experienced "good" and "not so good" authentication processes. Part of the problem is that others often make the decision as to the risk they are prepared to take in protecting your identity. Essentially, the financial services institution, government, healthcare provider or other organization with which you are dealing decide how they will authenticate your identity. You may have little say in the process.

The media frequently reports incidents that highlight how relatively easy it is for thieves to fraudulently replicate each of the many ways identity is authenticated. Whether authentication is done with a debit or credit card, SIN card or driver's licence or by true electronic means, such as a password or e-mail address, these all are opportunities for someone else to take these identifiers over and become you. The easiest way a thief can do this is to claim that there is a problem, for example, pretending to have forgotten the access code for your telephone banking.

The burgeoning use of the Internet further highlights authentication issues and poor practices. First, the Internet makes it very easy for someone to gather a great deal of personal and financial information about you as an individual. Second, there are many ways that an individual's identity may be authenticated online, including your having to provide personal information on the websites of enterprises about which you may know little, if anything. Third, the Internet allows faceless information thieves to masquerade as others to do such things as make an online application for credit in another person's name. Internet security issues are discussed in Chapters 13 to 15.

...

As incidents of fraud and identity theft continue to increase, you should expect authentication processes to become more stringent and for technology to be used more often. For example, biometric systems are already being used in Europe for simple transactions. Face image or eye retina scanners are now being used to verify the customer's identity at some ABMs.

PRACTICAL STEPS TO PROTECT YOURSELF
Authenticating Your Identity

- Ask the financial services institution, provider or organization to what extent you are allowed to manage the risk when authenticating your identity. Consider how easy and convenient the process is for you and how difficult is it for an impostor.
- If you are asked to provide your mother's maiden name, ask why the information is being collected and whether it will be verified. Where the provision of your mother's maiden name is not a legal requirement, consider using a creative adaptation of the name to make this identifier a viable security check that another person cannot replicate.
- Provide your SIN only when legally required. Ask to use other types of identification when possible.
- If you are concerned that the authentication process may not adequately protect your identity and your access to services, take your business elsewhere.

ASSESSING AND MINIMIZING YOUR COMPUTER AND ONLINE RISKS

9

How do you and your family use computers and the Internet? How much personal and financial information do you process and store on your hard drive? Do you use the computer for online banking or brokerage trading? Do you often use another computer to process personal and financial information when you are away from your home?

When you use a computer to process and store information and the Internet to search for information, send and receive e-mails, buy items or complete forms online, you do so voluntarily. These activities are a personal choice, as is the amount of risk you are prepared to take that your information may be disclosed and misused. Regardless of your level of usage, everyone who owns a personal computer or uses the Internet in any way needs to be prepared to accept some degree of risk.

What can go wrong?

The physical loss of your computer or invasion by a computerized (electronic) virus that destroys data or makes your computer unusable, are nasty accidents that can cause much inconvenience. Some of these "viruses" can capture your keystrokes or transfer files from your computer to a third party that has planted the malicious code on the computer you are using. You also need to be concerned about the potential abuses and losses if the wrong person accesses and uses the personal information you may have on your computer.

The *Practical Steps to Protect Yourself* throughout these chapters are the **precautions that everyone should take, regardless of how little or how much you use your personal computer and the Internet**. Following these steps will ensure that you have a fundamental level of control over your personal and financial information based on the risk inherent in your activities. This chapter provides an overview of the protective steps you need to implement; each of these topics is discussed more fully in the chapters that follow.

The Physical Loss of Your Computer

A thief will steal a computer to use it or to resell it. Consider also that the personal and financial information stored on your computer could be the primary motive for the theft.

Storing personal, financial and private information on alternate media, such as floppy disks, CD-ROMs, USB memory sticks, rather than on your computer's hard drive will reduce the damage caused by the loss of your computer and the exposure to your sensitive information.

Prying Eyes

Generally people simply do not want anyone (not just strangers but also family and friends) to be able to access, read or copy the personal information that they use online and may store on their computer. This would include private information such as e-mails, identification information, salaries, tax returns, bank balances, savings and investments.

Consider, however, just how many people may be able to access your computer files and any information you provide online. Children, friends, houseguests, visitors, babysitters, house cleaners, co-workers, the computer repairperson, hackers and your Internet service provider (ISP) are just some of the possible intruders. Of note is that the person who accesses and abuses a victim's personal information is often someone that the victim knows and trusts.

Here again if you store your personal, financial and private information on alternate media rather than on your computer's hard drive and password-protect these files, you will reduce the opportunity for prying eyes.

Misuse of Personal and Financial Information Provided Over the Internet

While many people commonly worry about their credit card number being disclosed or shared once provided online, you also need to be concerned about the privacy of your personal identity information.

When you subscribe to an online service, set up an e-mail service profile, make an online purchase or complete an electronic form online, you are often required to disclose personal, financial and private information over the Internet. In these instances, you need to be aware that others can access this information, either intentionally or unintentionally. Also consider that enterprises to which you voluntarily disclose this information may disclose it to others without your permission or knowledge.

Freeware, Viruses, Worms and Trojan Horses

Freeware, viruses, worms, spyware and Trojan Horses are other ways that your information may be disclosed, captured or destroyed and even make your computer unusable. Any files, e-mail attachments or software that comes from an unknown source or that someone plants on the computer you use could contain malicious code that can cause serious problems.

These "invaders" have the ability to:
- Read and copy your personal, financial and private information and send it over the Internet to another person.
- Capture your keystrokes when you are inputting sensitive information, such as your identifier/name and passwords, including those used for your online banking, all of which can be analyzed and used by someone else.
- Delete files, folders and potentially everything on your hard drive.
- Generally make your computer unstable and even unusable.

Consider also that software that is used to share and exchange files (e.g., music files) can have the ability to share other information from your computer. Defending yourself against viruses and other malicious code are discussed in Chapter 11.

A BASIC PROTECTION PLAN

The *Basic Protection Plan* establishes some fundamental steps to protect your computer, including if it is used to go online. The Plan is intended to ensure that everyone who uses your computer takes the basic steps needed to protect sensitive personal information and their online activities.

These steps are critical whether you use your computer or the Internet infrequently or constantly. If you use your personal computer and the Internet in a fairly restricted low-risk manner, you may find that this plan is all that you need.

However, if you are performing tasks on your computer that are at a higher level of risk, you should be taking additional steps to protect your money, privacy and identity. In this instance, you should use the plan as a model to create a *Personal Protection Plan* that reflects your customized or family protection plan and addresses specific areas of risk when you are computing and using the Internet.

PRACTICAL STEPS TO PROTECT YOURSELF
Establishing the Basic Protection Plan
This plan applies to everyone.

Your Personal Computer Protection (See Chapter 10.)
Use your computer's operating system and software security features (where available):
- Set up your computer so that you (and/or one other person) are the only person(s) who can install or remove software, make software changes, and add other components, e.g., a new printer.
- Set up an administrator and separate personal name/identifiers and passwords for all users and a guest identifier for visitors who may use your computer.
- Restrict your computer's guest password access to only very basic functions on your computer. Caution: Guest users may still be able to receive and open e-mail attachments unless your e-mail software is also password-protected.
- Enforce personal passwords and regular changes of passwords, including the guest password.
- Change all default values of supplied software and system passwords to your own selected password.
- Ensure that you keep up-to-date with operating system and browser security releases and patches. Use auto-detection capabilities, where available, to ensure you receive automatic notifications of updates and fixes.
- Use software passwords wherever available to control access to your information and software, e.g., for access to e-mail and financial management software.
- Do NOT use freeware software from an unknown source.

Your Electronic Identification Protection (See Chapter 10.)
- Select passwords and passphrases that are easy for you to remember and disguise, yet difficult for someone to guess or discover.
- Use passwords and passphrases that are at least seven characters long.
- Do not disclose your passwords to anyone and only record them in a disguised or hidden manner.
- Change your passwords and passphrases regularly.

Your Virus Protection (See Chapter 11.)
Acquire virus scanner software from a reputable vendor, register it, and:
- Keep the virus scanner current with new releases and fixes to your version.
- Regularly update your virus definition file.
- Configure the scanner to be active on start-up and to scan continuously in "background" mode, including when you open e-mail.
- Regularly scan your full system (all files, programs and hard drives) **at least once a month**.

- Scan all floppy disks and other removable media that you are given by someone else before you open them for use on your computer.
- Set the scanner to automatically notify you when there are online releases, new virus definitions and fixes to your version of the software.
- Consider updating you virus scanner each year, and when you change your operating system, to take advantage of new features that are more likely to be compatible with your operating system.

Your Information Protection (See Chapters 10 and 12.)

Use alternate media and software features to protect your personal, financial and private information:

- Store your personal, financial and private information on alternate media, NOT on your computer's hard drive. Alternate media includes floppy disks, CD-ROMs, storage tape drives, USB memory keys or sticks.
- Instruct your software, e.g., financial management software such as Quicken and Microsoft Money, to write your data files to the alternate media rather than to your computer's hard drive.
- Take a second, back-up copy of these information files in case the first one fails.
- Secure both the primary and back-up copies safely, but separately. One may be locked in a desk drawer, readily accessible to you. The other back-up copy should be stored in a fireproof safe or safety deposit box.

Your Computer Use Protection (See Chapters 10 and 12.)

Always log off, close down software and shut down your computer:

- Log off of any website that you have previously visited and/or logged onto.
- Close down your browser and other software when you have finished using them and before someone else uses them.
- Power down your computer by using "power saver" or "hibernation mode" when not in use for a period of time, e.g., 10 or 30 minutes, and require password re-entry to reactivate the computer.
- Turn off your computer when not in use for an extended period.

Your Disclosure Protection (See Chapters 13 and 14.)

- Take precautions when disclosing personal, financial or private information over the Internet when:
  - Giving such information
  - Buying products or services, and
  - Registering and using online services, such as MyServices, for creating a custom home page.
- Use only reputable websites to disclose personal, financial and private information.
- Only rely on the security practices (i.e., those with SSL or more advanced security) of your financial services institution, government sites and reputable merchants and service providers.

- Do NOT disclose personal, financial and private information.
  - On a personal or family website
  - To News Groups, Bulletin Boards or Chat Lines.
- Do NOT regularly and continuously use sensitive personal, financial or private information when computing online from another computer.

Your E-mail Protection (See Chapters 11 and 13.)

- Treat your e-mail like a postcard that can be read by anyone. Do NOT send e-mails containing sensitive personal, financial or private information unless you know it is safe, e.g., use encryption.
- Delete all spam e-mail without opening it. Do NOT react or respond to it, other than to inform your Internet Service Provider (ISP).

Your Information Highway Protection (See Chapter 14.)

- Be cautious when buying goods and services online and dealing with someone you have never met.
- Do NOT gamble online.
- Be selective and cautious as to the Internet websites that you visit and browse; treat them as you would a dark or blind alley when walking or driving.

ASSESSING THE LEVEL OF YOUR COMPUTER AND ONLINE RISK

Based on your computing and online computing usage, your risk exposure may be categorized as **low**, **moderate** or **high risk**.

The following is designed to help you do a comprehensive assessment of your specific computing and Internet activities relevant to the risk to your money, privacy and identity.

- Indicate your response, "yes" or "no" or N/A for not applicable, for each of the questions below.
- Be sure to consider the computing and online activities of the other members of your family or guests who may use your computer.
- Enter the corresponding L, M or H indicated in the far right column for those questions to which your response is "yes".

Your responses to these questions will help you determine whether your risks are generally low, moderate or high so that you can implement the necessary preventative steps for minimizing your risk, as discussed in greater detail in the chapters that follow.

Assessing Your Risks

YOUR CONNECTION TO THE INTERNET (INTERNET SERVICE PROVIDER OR ISP)	YES, NO or N/A	L, M or H
Dial-up Internet connection on telephone line		L
High-speed cable provider, e.g., Rogers		M
DSL (Digital Subscriber Line), e.g., Sympatico high speed on telephone line		M
Share connection to Internet — two or more computers are networked with cable or wireless hub		H
YOUR COMPUTER ACTIVITIES		
Usage		
Create word processing documents		L
Create spreadsheet documents and presentations		L
Manage personal finances using financial management software, e.g., Quicken, QuickBooks or Microsoft Money		M
Use mobile computing when away from your home or place of work		M
Browsing and Shopping on the Internet		
Visit websites that are not by their nature high risk		L
Visit adult websites or gambling sites		H
Search and gather information, by cutting and pasting		L
Download documents and images from reputable sites, e.g., CNN		M
Download and install software purchased from "reputable" websites		M
Download and install software and freeware from other websites (i.e., not known, reputable vendors)		H
Complete simple online forms, e.g., register for contests		M
Complete financial online forms, e.g., loan and mortgage applications		H
Occasionally buy products using a credit card from "reputable" sites[1]		M
Buy products using a credit card from other websites		H
Access Chat Rooms		H
Share/exchange video, program and music files		H

[1] Reputable websites, such as Sears or Indigo, are generally secure sites. For example, the site will state it is secure and may have a lock icon or other symbol at the bottom of the screen. If you click on this icon, the SSL or Secure Socket Layer certification pops up to verify the site uses high encryption to protect your private information. Or the site may use other more advanced security. This is discussed in Chapter 14.

	YES, NO or N/A	L, M or H
Online Banking		
Make basic transfers and payments and view account records		M
Download data to reconcile financial accounts		M
Do brokerage trading of investments		H
E-mail		
Occasionally send and receive personal e-mails		L
Regularly send and receive e-mails, occasionally with word processing attachments		M
Receive e-mails with word processing, spreadsheet and/or image files		M
Receive e-mail attachments with executable code, e.g., programs, jokes		H
Computer Games		
Play games purchased and installed on computer		L
Play games over the Internet		M
Play games given to you on a disk or CD-ROM or downloaded from freeware sites		H

What is Your Level of Risk?

If your score on the chart above shows that your activities are predominantly Ls, you are generally a low-risk user. The Ms indicate a moderate risk and Hs a high risk. Of course, you may have activities on all three levels and should therefore consider adopting the Practical Steps relevant to the risk level of the specific activities, as outlined on the chart that follows.

REDUCING YOUR RISKS

Now that you have generally assessed your level of risk, you can take active steps to reduce your risks when computing and going online as well as protect the most sensitive personal information that you want to store and use on your personal computer.

The checklist that follows is divided into two sections detailing the protection steps to be taken by moderate and high-risk users:
- If you are a moderate-risk user, complete the *Basic Protection Plan* explained earlier in this chapter and the first section of the Practical Steps below.
- If you are a high-risk user, complete the *Basic Protection Plan* explained earlier in this chapter and the two sections of the Practical Steps below.

Do not be concerned if at this point you do not fully understand each of the steps you need to take. The steps are cross-referenced to topics discussed in later chapters where you will find explanations and further information about the steps you can take to protect your money, privacy and identity.

PRACTICAL STEPS TO PROTECT YOURSELF
Moderate Risk:
Additional Steps to the Basic Protection Plan
- Regularly virus scan your full system, **once a week**. (See Chapter 11.)
- Regularly clear your cache, Internet Temporary Files, history files and AutoComplete history of forms and passwords each time you close your browser software. (See Chapter 15.)
- Configure your browser software to NOT save user names (IDs) and passwords; also consider controlling cookies, Java and Active-X. (See Chapter 15.)
- Consider installing a personal software firewall that allows you to restrict online activity to just those activities you select, including restricting access to the Internet from your computer. (See Chapter 15.)
- Configure the firewall for your Internet activity and review its settings regularly. (See Chapter 15.)

High Risk:
Additional Steps to the Basic Protection Plan and Moderate Risk
- Install a hardware firewall (in addition to your software firewall); this is essential where you use a network of computers (LAN). (See Chapter 15.)
- Integrate the hardware firewall, your "personal" firewall software and virus scanner to ensure all are present and active when you are online. (See Chapter 15.)
- Virus scan your full system often, at least weekly, depending on how frequently you:
  — Use the Internet,
  — Download software, and/or
  — Open e-mail attachments.
  (See Chapter 11.)
- Isolate and quarantine spam and other suspicious e-mails and attachments before opening them. (See Chapter 14.)
- Do not use file-sharing software. If you or your family must share files over the Internet with "strangers," establish a separate partition on your hard drive, to download file-sharing software and shared files. (See also Chapter 13.)
- Consider using software utilities to automatically manage cache, Internet Temporary Files, history files, cookies, Active-X, etc. (See Chapter 15.)

- Consider encrypting sensitive files, sensitive e-mails and data. (See Chapter 15.)
- Do NOT communicate personal, financial or private information/images on an unencrypted wireless local area network (WLAN) at home, your place of work or when travelling. (See Chapter 15.)

YOUR PERSONAL PROTECTION PLAN

Regardless of your level of risk, everyone should apply the practical protect your-self steps in the *Basic Protection Plan*. The next step is to adopt the specific additional protection steps that apply to your risk assessment and activities to create a customized *Personal Protection Plan* for you and your family. Your *Personal Protection Plan* should reflect your assessed level of risk and the nature of your activities. You should regularly review your risk assessment and modify your *Personal Protection Plan* as your computing and online activities and risks change.

Implementing these practical steps to protect yourself and your activities will involve an investment of time and some inconvenience. However, when you consider the cost and time to recover from an accident or intrusion, the time is well spent.

PRACTICAL STEPS TO PROTECT YOURSELF
Establishing Your Personal Protection Plan

- Develop a customized *Personal Protection Plan* for you and your family based on your assessed level of risk and the nature of your computing and online activities, and including the steps above for moderate and high-risk activities.
- Regularly reassess your computing and online activities and associated risks, say every six months, or when you buy a new computer or change your ISP.
- Revise your family's *Personal Protection Plan* to reflect your changes in your risk assessment and activities.

GETTING THE SUPPORT OF EVERYONE

Much of this book teaches life-skills for which there is no school program and no proficiency test except for learning from experience and perhaps the occasional computer crash. The young are not intimidated by technology and will explore its capabilities and solve problems intuitively. Their approach is often: "what can this technology do for me?" Older generations may use computers with trepidation and less intuition and be more likely to refer to manuals.

Regardless of the age of the computer or online user, you need to ensure that each and every person that accesses your computer understands the steps that must be taken to protect the computer and any information that is stored on it. You need to review the accidents that can happen, help them understand the risks and get their commitment to use the computer safely and properly.

PRACTICAL STEPS TO PROTECT YOURSELF
Setting Out the Steps that Everyone Needs to Take

- Lead by example. Ensure every user consistently and persistently follows your *Personal Protection Plan.*
- Do NOT disclose personal, financial and private information online, especially on a personal or family website or to News Groups, Bulletin Boards, or Chat Lines.
- Do NOT disable password checkers, virus scanners and firewalls.
- Do NOT download freeware from unknown sources.
- Do NOT open e-mail from an unknown source with an attachment.
- Do NOT buy items online from someone you have never met, unless from a reputable merchant, auction site or individual.
- Do NOT gamble online.
- Do NOT let others, e.g., visitors or your children's friends, use the family computer unsupervised.

10

PROTECTING YOUR COMPUTER AND DATA

Your computer hardware, software and data need to be protected, regardless of whether you use the Internet. Like many users, you may have a great deal of personal information stored on the hard drive of your computer. The sensitivity of this information will vary. Some may be concerned about the privacy of the personal information in their e-mail, while others may have greater concerns about the data in their financial management program. In addition to the files that you create, you also have to be concerned that this information may be stored in Temporary Internet Files and back-up files that some applications create automatically.

MANAGING THE USE OF YOUR PERSONAL COMPUTER

Perhaps your computer is truly a personal computer, used exclusively by you. Perhaps your family, including your children and their friends who visit your home, use your computer and the Internet to access their e-mail, complete homework assignments, play games and download music and games.

Anyone who uses your computer and anyone who is able to access or steal your computer can read and misuse the personal and financial information you have stored on it, unless you take steps to protect it. If your computer is connected to the Internet, there are additional concerns that you need to think about and act on. Other users may not know all of the protection steps and rules set out in this book. They may go to Internet sites that are less than desirable, sites where viruses could be downloaded to your computer or they undertake other careless activities that could jeopardize the security of the information stored on your computer.

Low to High Risk

Your risk is low to moderate if you ensure all users understand and practice the practical measures in your *Personal Protection Plan*. You also need to monitor and control the activities of other users on your computer. If you let others use your computer indiscriminately and without guidelines, your risk is high.

PRACTICAL STEPS TO PROTECT YOURSELF
Managing the Use of Your Personal Computer

- Set out guidelines and boundaries. You may want to tell others that your computer is your personal property and nobody else is to use it. You may allow others to use your computer; however, you must make it very clear that they must NOT download anything from the Internet, load software or use disks that other people have given them.

- Inform others that if they wish to download from the Internet to your computer, you will decide if it is appropriate and safe and may download it for them but they are not to do it on their own. This is especially applicable if your children and their friends use the computer.

- Make every user aware of your *Personal Protection Plan*. Many of these steps will restrict others from using certain applications or files on your computer, such as assigning personal identifiers (IDs) and passwords. These are discussed later in this chapter. The steps in this plan can also help prevent others from participating in activities that could result in a virus infection or other problems. Viruses and other invaders are discussed in Chapter 11.

PROTECTING INFORMATION ON YOUR COMPUTER

What information do you store on your computer and where do you store it? These files could include letters, documents, pictures, graphics, presentations and other personal data that you create and save. However, you may not be aware that the software you use may also store information for later access on your computer or on another computer you may be using.

How does this happen? Some software applications allow you to set an option for making automatic back-up copies of your work while other applications may do this in the background without your knowledge. For example, the settings in your word processing software may automatically make a copy of the document you are opening that you can revert back to later, if necessary. Or they may be set to automatically make intermediate back-ups of the file (e.g., every 10 minutes). This latter feature means that your work and changes are not lost if the computer crashes while you are working on the document. You can usually decide where these back-up files are stored. They may default to an obscure folder, although one that a knowledgeable person could easily locate.

Similarly, your financial management software may automatically save and store back-up copies each time you add new data to your financial records. You should be familiar with the location of these stored files and periodically take steps to delete any files that you no longer need or use. These back-up copies should be recorded to removable media and the hard drive copy deleted.

Do not forget your "Temp" folder. Back-up copies of work are written to this temporary folder in certain applications whenever you download or open an e-mail attachment. The file is stored in the "Temp" folder on your hard drive until you specifically delete or clear it using certain system commands. The "Temp" files are particularly a concern when you use another computer, as you could unknowingly leave personal data on the computer that others could access.

Low to High Risk

To lower your risk, be aware of the automatic back-up and temporary file features of your computer programs and periodically delete files that you no longer need or use. Use alternate removable media, such as floppy disks or CD-ROMs, to store sensitive information (rather than storing it on your hard drive) to lower your risk, as discussed later in this chapter.

PRACTICAL STEPS TO PROTECT YOURSELF
Managing the Storage of Data Files

- Determine where personal, financial and private information is stored on your computer and how and when it is copied and/or backed up. This should include back-up copies that your financial management software may automatically save. Make sure you know the location of these back-up files and after backing them up to alternate media, delete the files from your hard drive that you no longer need or use.
- When you use another computer for personal use, be sure that you know what you are leaving behind you. This includes automatic back-up copies of word processing documents, e-mail attachments opened to a temporary file and browser cache files. Review the settings and options in the software you use to find where the information is stored even temporarily and delete it. Be sure to empty the Recycling Bin and browser cache when you have finished.

PHYSICAL PROTECTION OF YOUR COMPUTER AND DATA

If your computer were stolen or lost, presumably it is insured. The more critical concern is that someone could access the personal, financial and private information you have stored on your hard drive. This data could be of more value to the thief than the computer itself, and may indeed be the primary reason for the theft.

Low to High Risk

If you are a high-risk user, a thief could potentially find out a great deal about you. For example, if you store personal information about yourself and your family on your computer, much of this could be used in conjunction with standard software, such as personal financial management software to steal your money, privacy and identity. This includes information such as names, addresses, birth dates, mothers' maiden names, the family tree, financial account numbers, credit card numbers and health records. If you take steps to store this information on alternate removable media, your risk is low, as discussed later.

Also at risk are the files that you may keep with lists of your passwords, bankcard and credit card numbers, the activation code to your home alarm system, the combination for your safe, and your SIN and passport numbers. You may keep this data in a secret file that you think no one can find; however, a skilled thief can find this information. It may be easier to access than you realize if you regularly access this file and it is automatically added to your computer's favourites or documents tabs.

Protecting Your Personal Data

The easiest and simplest way to protect your personal sensitive information from the prying eyes of other users and from thieves who want to steal your money or identity is to NOT store this sensitive information on the hard drive. Instead it should be stored on alternate media such as a floppy disk, CD-ROM, USB memory key or some other removable storage medium, all of which are relatively inexpensive.

You also need to set the automatic back-up feature of software such as your word processing and financial management applications so that these back-up files are only stored on the removable medium and not on your hard drive. Be sure to create a second, back-up copy of all your data files in case the first one fails.

Alternatively, consider a more technical step. Use encryption software to encrypt all files that contain sensitive information and prevent unauthorized access. Encryption is discussed in Chapter 15.

PRACTICAL STEPS TO PROTECT YOURSELF
Protecting Your Personal Computer and Information

- Regularly review the uses of your computer and the personal, financial or private information about you and your family that you may store on it.

- Review your *Personal Protection Plan* and adjust your practical steps to reflect any new risk exposures. Inform all users of any additional precautions that they are to take when using the computer.
- Use the computer's system security features to require log on with a personal ID and password. System security features are discussed later in this chapter.
- Do NOT store sensitive personal and financial information on your hard drive (or keep automatic back-up copies there) that can be accessed by the casual user of your computer, or friend. Consider also that when you send your computer out for upgrades or repairs, a technician could access these files.
- Store your personal, financial and private information on alternate removable media, **not** your computer's hard drive. Alternate media include floppy disks, CD-ROMs, storage tape drives, USB memory keys or sticks or some other removable storage medium.
- Instruct your software, e.g., financial management software such as Quicken and Microsoft Money, to write your data files to the alternate media rather than your computer's hard drive.
- Take a second back-up copy of these data files in case the first one fails.
- Secure both copies safely, but separately. One may be locked in a desk drawer, readily accessible to you. The other back-up copy should be stored securely in a fireproof safe or safety deposit box.
- Physically safeguard your laptop computer at all times, particularly when travelling.

Technical step to consider:
- If you need to store sensitive personal and financial information on your hard drive, use encryption software to prevent unauthorized access.

YOUR OPERATING SYSTEM'S SECURITY FEATURES

Increasingly, computer operating systems such as Windows 2000 and higher versions include system security features that are easy to configure and can add valuable protection to the information you store on your computer.

The Administrator

One important feature is that you can set up an administrator for the computer. Usually this person is the only user who can set up capabilities and security controls for other users. The feature also lets you restrict other users' actions by limiting their access to files and/or programs on your computer.

For example, the administrator may set up the system so that:
- All users must log on to the computer with their name and personal password.
- Users must change their passwords periodically, such as every 30 days.

- The administrator is the only one who can add and delete components, e.g., software. So while everyone may be able to download software (but should be cautioned not to do this), only the administrator can install it.
- Temporary users must use a guest identifier that limits their computing capabilities on the system, even restricting the printing of documents.

Screen Saver, Sleep or Hibernation Mode

Your operating system should have features for setting up a screen saver, sleep mode or hibernation mode that the computer activates automatically when it is not in use for a prolonged period. Your computer should let you set the:

- Timeframes for these modes to be activated, such as after 10 or 30 minutes, and
- Password access to reactivate the computer from the screen saver, sleep or hibernation mode.

These protective steps are particularly important where your computer is continuously connected to the Internet, e.g., with cable or DSL. Use the password access of these features to prevent others from using your computer to access the Internet. Screen saver, sleep and hibernation mode may not prevent access to the Internet, depending on your particular model of computer and software.

Low to High Risk

Using your operating system's security features can help you manage users' activities on your computer by determining who has access and what they can and cannot do. Help features and some trial and error will ensure some protection for your computer.

A word of caution: If your computer is stolen or accessed by an intruder, a knowledgeable person could override many of these security features by using a boot disk to restart the computer. Consider encrypting sensitive information. Encryption is discussed in Chapter 15.

PRACTICAL STEPS TO PROTECT YOURSELF
Using Your Operating System's Security Features

- Become familiar with your computer system security features and implement them commensurate with your assessment of your risk.
- Set up your computer so that you (and/or one other person) are the only person(s) who can install or remove software, make software changes, and add other components, e.g., a new printer.

- Set up an administrator and separate personal name/identifiers and passwords for all users and a guest identifier for visitors who may use your computer.
- Restrict your computer's guest password access to only very basic functions on your computer. Caution: Guest users may still be able to receive and open e-mail attachments unless your e-mail software is also password-protected.
- Enforce the use of personal passwords and change them regularly. Create a separate password for guest users.
- Set up your computer to go into screen saver, sleep or hibernation mode when your computer is not in use (e.g., after 10 or 30 minutes of inactivity). This feature is discussed later in this chapter.
- Set up your computer so that a password is required to reactivate your computer when the screen saver, sleep or hibernation mode has been activated.

SYSTEM AND SOFTWARE PASSWORDS

Your operating system and computer software likely have many capabilities for you to use passwords, other than just when you log in, but typically few people use them. Many people feel they have too many already, so why create more? However, these passwords are an additional measure for protecting your money, privacy and identity and since the capability is included with the software, they can be activated at no additional cost.

You should also become familiar with the default passwords that may exist on your computer and its software and ensure that you change all default passwords supplied by the vendor to your own unique passwords.

Screen Savers, Hibernation and Sleep Mode

As previously discussed, the screen saver, sleep or hibernation mode allows you to prevent others from using your computer when you are not using it. The operating system gives you the option of setting a password to reactivate your computer after it has timed out. Therefore, you can set your computer to automatically go to screen saver mode after a period time, e.g., 10 minutes, and require that the correct password be entered before the computer is reactivated from this mode. You can set this password as your log-in password that you use when you start up the computer.

E-mail

Some e-mail software gives you the ability to password-protect access to your e-mail. Being able to set your own password would prevent someone else from using your personal computer and accessing and browsing through your personal e-mail. Without the password, prying eyes could simply open the software to read all your e-mail as well as possibly send e-mail as if you were the sender.

Financial Management Software

Programs such as Quicken, QuickBooks, and Microsoft Money offer the capability to set passwords to open the files with your personal and financial information and to prevent others from using the software to access your information. This software helps you record and track your income, expenses, mortgage, loans, investments, insurance and other financial records such as an inventory of your home or safety deposit box. You may also include information about your financial account and credit card numbers and contacts, such as your representative at your financial services institution, stockbroker and insurance broker.

Additionally, the software will let you link to your accounts online to simplify your account balancing process or assess the value of your investment portfolio. As it is likely that you would not want other users to see this information, password protection is essential. You should also consider using alternate media to store these data files and back-up copies, as previously discussed, rather than store this sensitive information on your hard drive.

Income Tax Return Software

The password protection on tax return software prevents others using the software to access your tax returns. The software helps you to complete your annual income tax return; some programs even allow you to file your return electronically. As your return includes sensitive, personal information about you, not just your name, address and income but also information such as your SIN, date of birth, political preference, charitable gifts, health expenditures, investment income, and capital gains, password protection is essential to protect this data.

As you likely use this file only once a year, consider storing this sensitive data on alternate removable media and not on your hard drive. For example, copy it to a disk or CD-ROM when you have submitted your return, then delete the file from your hard drive to prevent someone from accessing it.

Word Processing

Many popular word processing packages and similar software let you seal a document or file by using a password such that only the person with the password can load the document or electronic form and read or amend it. This is a useful feature when sharing documents but caution should be used. The data may still be readable by other software programs.

PRACTICAL STEPS TO PROTECT YOURSELF
Managing System and Software Passwords
- Change all default passwords on software programs to passwords that you have personally selected.
- Configure your computer to go into a screen saver, hibernation or sleep mode when not in use for a period of time, e.g., 10 minutes, and require password re-entry to reactivate the computer.
- Use passwords wherever available to control access to your information and software, particularly e-mail, financial management and income tax return software.

Selecting Passwords and Passphrases
Generally passwords are a stronger form of electronic identification than PINs and access codes, particularly if you use passwords that include at least seven letters and numbers (including upper and lower cases) and change them regularly.

There are many ways to select passwords, but generally passphrases are easier to remember and can be written down in such a way that they cannot be easily deciphered. As there are no magic solutions or best approach to creating a passphrase, consider developing your own method. For example, use the first letter of each word in a line from a favourite song. The Resources section of this book includes suggestions and tips for creating your own unique passwords and passphrases.

Low to High Risk
Passwords and passphrases can help protect access to your personal information. To be effective, the passwords must be unique and you should not disclose them to anyone. Be sure to change them regularly.

PRACTICAL STEPS TO PROTECT YOURSELF
Selecting Strong Passwords and Passphrases
- Apply the tips and tricks provided in the Resources section to create unique passwords and passphrases.
- Only use passwords and passphrases that you have selected personally, wherever possible.
- Select passwords and passphrases that are easy for you to remember and disguise, yet difficult for someone else to guess.

- Where possible, use passwords and passphrases that include at least seven characters and/or numbers.
- Change your passwords and passphrases regularly, where possible.

BACK-UPS

Backing up the information on your computer regularly and keeping the back-up copies in a safe place should be a regular routine for every computer user. Some people regularly do full system back-up copies of all their data, software and programs. Others create back-up copies of only their most important files and e-mail.

Safeguard your back-up files as you would the original files. Secure the back-up copy by placing it a sealed envelope or similar container and store it in a secure place such as in a safe, safety deposit box, locked desk drawer or locked filing cabinet.

As an additional measure, encrypt all sensitive information, including the information on your back-ups, to ensure there is little chance of someone accessing this information. Encryption is discussed in Chapter 15.

PRACTICAL STEPS TO PROTECT YOURSELF
Managing Back-ups
- Regularly back up your files and folders and be sure to safeguard back-up copies of personal, financial or private information as you would the original files.

Technical step to consider:
- Encrypt your back-up data files.

DELETING FILES

A common misconception is that when a file or document is deleted from a computer, it is permanently deleted. This is usually not the case. Generally deleting simply means assigning the file or document to the Recycle Bin, trash, or equivalent. The file is simply re-indexed and assigned for deletion/reuse but is generally recoverable for a period of time.

Further, when you instruct the computer to empty the Recycling Bin or equivalent, it may simply delete the entry in the index to the file or document and not the original file. The actual bits and bytes that electronically constitute your personal or financial information may still be recoverable from the hard drive or disk using data recovery software.

One way to overcome this is to regularly defrag your hard-drive. Defragmentation is a process by which your operating system or a special software program defragments your hard drive so that your computer runs faster and more efficiently. Your computer's operating system includes a disk defragmenter utility program. Use the Help feature to locate the function and instructions on how to use it. However, as defragmentation may take several hours to complete, do this task when you do not need the computer for any other purpose.

An alternative way to protect your personal files is to encrypt them before you delete them, then delete the encrypted files and immediately empty the Recycling Bin.

Do not forget your e-mail software. Many people simply keep all of their e-mail and do not routinely delete e-mails that are no longer needed. If you need to save the content of an e-mail, cut/paste it into your word processing program, save it as a file, and delete the original e-mail. If it is sensitive information, encrypt the file.

When you delete old e-mail messages, they are sent to the trash bin within your e-mail software. You then need to empty the trash. Use the Help function for an explanation of how to do this in your e-mail program.

PRACTICAL STEPS TO PROTECT YOURSELF
Protecting Deleted Information
- Carefully ensure that all files and e-mails containing personal, financial or private information are deleted and not just recycled.
- Run the disk defragmentation utility periodically, e.g., every six months.

SOFTWARE PATCHES AND FIXES
Safe computing includes using registered (not pirated) software and doing regularly maintenance, the same way you maintain a car. Software vendors regularly provide patches and fixes to problems identified after the release in addition to the new versions of their software. As many of these patches, fixes and releases relate to security issues, you should install them where they affect your software.

Make it a regular habit to check for new or updated releases, patches or fixes to your operating system, browser and software programs. Link online to the appropriate website or call the vendor's 1-800 number. The website should assist you in identifying patches and new releases. Some websites ask you to allow them to run an online diagnostic test of your computer to determine which releases, patches and fixes your program needs. Simply follow the installation instructions. Many of these changes are self-installing and do not need your intervention once you click on the download icon.

Some software programs have auto-detection capabilities that automatically detect and download patches and fixes to your computer (e.g., Windows and Internet Explorer) over the Internet. A pop-up window notifies you when these are available. However, do not automatically install patches and fixes without first reviewing them and then selecting those that you require.

Whenever you install new releases of your operating system or browser, make sure your virus scanner's automatic detection is activated. Additionally, run your virus scanner each time you have installed software patches, fixes or upgrades. Virus scanners are discussed in Chapter 11.

Low Risk

If updates, patches and fixes are downloaded from the vendor's site or you purchase the new release on a sealed CD-ROM, you can be reasonably assured that the code is genuine and authentic.

PRACTICAL STEPS TO PROTECT YOURSELF
Managing Software Updates, Patches and Fixes

- Keep your operating system and browser security up-to-date with releases and patches.
- Register your software and regularly (e.g., every three months) check for new releases, patches and fixes, particularly those that relate to security. Install these software code changes under virus scanner protection.
- Use software auto-detection capabilities, where available, to identify new patches, fixes and releases.

11

DEFENDING YOUR
COMPUTER AGAINST VIRUSES
AND OTHER INVADERS

Malicious code is an issue for all computer users. Viruses, worms, Trojan horses and other invaders can be transmitted on floppy disks, CD-ROMs and software programs as well as through e-mail, downloading and hacker abuse. These invaders are commonly referred to as malware, meaning malicious code or software. For the purposes of this discussion, the term virus includes all malware, worms, Trojan horses and other such invaders.

Viruses that invade your computer may run automatically or be triggered to execute on start-up of your computer or some other activity, such as a date of the year. You may not even know that the virus is on your computer until the accident happens.

Generally, your computer can be infected with a virus by:
- A malicious person who has physical access to your computer
- Loading software that includes an infection, often freeware and games
- Downloading software, documents and images from a website
- Using file-sharing software
- Sharing disks
- A hacker accessing your computer over the Internet, or
- An infected or malicious e-mail attachment.

The impact of a virus on your computer and the information stored there can vary widely. Some of these invaders are benign and may just activate a pop-up screen with a greeting or a joke. Others may be capable of deleting the contents of your hard drive or capturing personal information that could put your money, privacy and identity at risk. The Internet provides electronic communications access to your computer that can make virus infection easier and could even result in information being retrieved and sent from your computer over the Internet to the invader without your knowledge.

E-MAIL

For most low-risk users of the Internet, the e-mail vehicle is the most likely way that your computer can become infected by malicious code. The viruses are usually caught when you open an attachment from an unknown source.

Sometimes the e-mail attachment masquerades as a useful tool or is an appealing picture, image or joke. When you click and open it, this action will either launch or download the virus or immediately activate it. In some e-mail programs, a virus in an attachment can be triggered simply by viewing the e-mail in a split-screen preview mode, i.e., where the top half of the screen contains the list of e-mails while the bottom half of the screen shows the contents of the e-mail that is highlighted in the top half of the screen. Other viruses may be triggered by other events, such as a specific date and time, e.g., when Friday falls on the 13th of the month.

Most e-mail software packages can be configured to work with your virus scanner to protect your system from viruses as well as suppress spamming. Virus scanners are discussed later in this chapter. Integration of the virus scanner software and your e-mail software ensures that all e-mails and attachments are virus scanned as they arrive at your computer and when opened or downloaded. You should ensure that you are able to configure the software to also scan zipped files, a file compression format that is commonly used for e-mail attachments.

The Suspicious E-mail

What do you do if you receive a suspicious e-mail from someone you know? A suspicious e-mail is one that it is out of character and not what you would expect from the sender, such as an e-mail from your employer or ex-spouse with the subject line "I Love You". This type of e-mail can originate from a worm code that sends the e-mail to everyone in the electronic address book of the sender's computer. However, it may be legitimate e-mail. To safely handle this type of e-mail, do not open it and do not click on reply. Send a new e-mail to the sender or telephone the person to confirm that the e-mail is legitimate and safe to open.

Low Risk to High Risk

E-mail is generally a low-risk activity if you take the proper preventative measures and have installed a virus scanner on your system.

PRACTICAL STEPS TO PROTECT YOURSELF
Using E-mail

- Treat your e-mail like a postcard that can be read by anyone. Do NOT send e-mails containing your most sensitive personal, financial or private information unless you know the transmission is secure, e.g., you use encryption.
- Delete all spam e-mail without opening it. Do NOT react or respond to it.
- Do NOT open attachments and e-mail from unknown or suspicious sources.

Technical step to consider:
• Integrate your e-mail and virus scanner to ensure all e-mail is automatically scanned.

VIRUS SCANNERS

Virus scanners are software programs that can be purchased or downloaded online. They work to prevent and detect viruses and help eliminate them if viruses are detected on your computer. Norton and McAfee are two popular programs; there are many other reputable virus scanner programs on the market. You may also want to find out if your employer has a virus scanner licensing agreement that would extend its use to your home computer.

Every computer and Internet user should install virus scanner software. You only need one piece of software to work with all known viruses as long as it is kept current with releases and fixes for your version and updates of the latest definitions of new viruses. The software package can be purchased from a computer store or online at the vendor's website and downloaded immediately. Virus scanner software is easy to install and configure. The programs also include Help functions to guide you.

Generally, your protective measures should include the following:
• Make sure your virus scanner is the latest version. Purchase the program or download it from the vendor's website. A standard feature of most virus scanner software is to automatically notify you of releases and fixes and to install them for you, either on your instructions or automatically.
• Register online as a user of the virus scanner software so you can update automatically.
• Activate the scanner's auto-detect feature and ensure it continues working. This auto-detect causes the scanner to run automatically when you start your computer and continuously in the background to check for viruses infections and activations. If the program discovers a virus, it alerts you and quarantines it. Carefully follow the scanner's instructions on how to proceed.
• Activate the virus scanner's automated schedulers to periodically do a full system scan for viruses, including your hard drive, programs and files. Schedule it to run at times when you are not normally using the computer, but it is powered up and the operating system is active, e.g., on a Friday evening. How frequently you do a full system scan depends on how frequently you use your computer and your risk assessment (based on the chart you completed in Chapter 9). At a minimum, schedule a full system scan once a month, but if you and your family are frequent users of the Internet, downloading music and swapping files, scan at least once a week.

- Regularly check your scanner software, e.g., monthly, to ensure it is working in background mode as required, has been updated recently for the new virus definitions and has performed the scheduled full system scan on schedule.

Low to High Risk

Computer viruses are generally transmitted through the software you or your family install or download to your computer and often through connections that you regularly use, such as your e-mail. Viruses can be a very serious accident but if you are well prepared, a virus could simply be the equivalent of a scratch. Following the preventative measures discussed here will greatly reduce your risk of virus infections and protect your money, privacy and identity.

PRACTICAL STEPS TO PROTECT YOURSELF
Protecting Your Computer with a Virus Scanner

- Acquire virus scanner software from a reputable vendor and register it.
- Keep the virus scanner current with new releases and fixes to your version.
- Regularly update your virus definition file.
- Configure the scanner to be active on start-up and to scan continuously in "background" mode, including when you open e-mail.
- Regularly scan your full system (all files, programs and hard drives) **at least once a month**.
- Scan all floppy disks and other removable media that you are given by someone else before you open them for use on your computer.
- Set the scanner to automatically notify you when there are online releases, new virus definitions and fixes to your version of the software.
- Consider updating your virus scanner each year, and when you change your operating system, to take advantage of new features that are more likely to be compatible with your operating system.
- If your virus scanner software detects a virus infection, carefully follow the scanner's instructions for dealing with it.

Technical step to consider:

- Integrate your virus scanner with your hardware firewall to ensure that virus checking is automatically present while online traffic is being allowed. Firewalls are discussed in Chapter 15.

HACKERS

The Internet not only makes it easy for you to connect and surf, but once you are connected, others can attempt to access your computer and your information. These uninvited visitors are commonly known as hackers.

The hacker moniker is not limited to the teenager looking for adventure. Increasingly, hackers include organized groups intent on invading not just your computer but also your privacy as they seek information about your identity and access to any financial records you may have stored on your computer. They may even plant code on your personal computer that will report back details of a debit card number and password when you do online banking. Current virus scanner software can help protect against much hacker activity, particularly where they plant known software on your computer.

Low to High Risk
Hackers may get information about you not just from your computer but also from another computer or server that has processed your browser request or supports a website you have visited. Generally, hackers target business systems more often than home computers. You may have read media reports of entire databases of information, such as credit card numbers, being accessed and copied by hackers.

PRACTICAL STEPS TO PROTECT YOURSELF
Protecting Your Computer from Hackers
* Disconnect from the Internet when you are not using it. Log off any website on which you have had to log on. Shut down your computer when it is not in use.

Technical step to consider:
* Install software and hardware firewalls.

SPAMMING

While less offensive and dangerous than the work of hackers, e-mail spamming is an annoying Internet activity. Generally, spamming is the widespread distribution of unsolicited e-mails.

Many of these e-mails are sent to advertise products and services and are similar to junk mail and faxes. However, some of these e-mails may have a more dangerous intent such as spreading virus infections through attachments or collecting e-mail addresses and other personal information that you have stored on your computer. Spammers can also create traffic jams (also referred to as "denial of service") by flooding ISPs with messages.

Configuring Your E-mail System

Many e-mail software packages allow you configure your "in box" to block spam mail. This may include automatically deleting mail that you have not received from that user before, or simply routing the mail to a separate "in box" for you to review later. The latter approach is obviously the safest, as an e-mail from a friend with a new e-mail address might otherwise be deleted.

Increasingly, third party commercial services are being offered to help you manage spam e-mail automatically. For example, these services may filter your e-mail to receive only messages from known persons in your address book.

> **Low Risk**
> Generally e-mail spam is a nuisance rather than a significant risk to your money, privacy and identity.

PRACTICAL STEPS TO PROTECT YOURSELF
Dealing with Spam E-mail

- Delete all spam e-mail without opening it. Do NOT react or respond to it other than to tell your ISP.

Technical steps to consider:

- Set your software to isolate and quarantine spam and other suspicious e-mails and e-mail attachments automatically before you open and examine them.
- Configure your e-mail software to work with your virus scanner to protect your system from viruses as well as to suppress spamming.
- Consider using a third party service to manage incoming messages.

SPYWARE (AND ADWARE)

Many websites would like to know more about your computer and Internet usage behaviours and activities. Periodically you may experience having a "pop-up" screen appear when using your browser. This intrusion may be a type of Trojan horse program that while it pretends to do one thing, may also be doing something else, such as tracking your browsing and reporting it back to someone without your knowledge. One well-known example pretends to be an online lottery game with "pop-up" advertisements that actually spy on your Internet activity. Some of the spyware even asks you to agree to a user licence and is copyrighted. Generally, spyware is not considered to be malicious to your computer, thus virus scanners do not look for it nor report its existence on your computer.

Increasingly, spyware detection software has become available that scans your computer and can automatically clean-up unwanted spyware (and adware). These scanners work in a similar manner to virus scanners and need to be regularly updated to remain current.

PRACTICAL STEPS TO PROTECT YOURSELF
Dealing with Spyware (and Adware)
- If a pop-up screen offers a free download of software, close it. Do not click "yes" to download any software unless you know what it is and you know that it is from a trusted website. The pop-up screen is sometimes titled Security Warning so as to trick you to run the program.
- Acquire spyware detection software and manage it in a similar manner to your virus scanning software.

12

CONNECTING
TO THE INTERNET

The ability for people to communicate and get news and information virtually instantly has changed dramatically in the past 50 years. This great modern-day Elizabethan era will likely go down in history as a time of revolutionary breakthroughs in communications and information sharing.

In the last decade, the Internet in particular has rapidly evolved to provide unprecedented easy access and opportunities for enterprises, governments, and individuals. Many people may wonder how they ever managed without the ability to go online as part of their everyday lives. At the same time, there are still people who have never used the worldwide Web. They go about their daily lives without the need for e-mail and browsers or the added stress that these technologies often bring.

The Internet is a vast, complex network of services, servers and information sources widely available and used by hundreds of millions of people around the world every day. It includes telecommunication carriers, Internet Service Providers (ISPs), enterprises, governments, universities and research institutes... and you as a user.

When you are on the Internet, your online request is routed through the servers, routers and switches that form the electronic backbone of the worldwide Web (WWW). If you trace the routing of a message electronically, you may be surprised at how many unknown intermediary parties are involved as your information travels across the Internet.

Whether you connect online infrequently or constantly, you need to be aware of the specific risks and benefits the Internet vehicles present and the ways that you can limit your risk when driving the information highway.

YOUR INTERNET SERVICE PROVIDER (ISP)

Generally individual users connect to the Internet through an ISP (Internet Service Provider). The ISP may also provide the user with an e-mail address. The ISP connection could be dial-up or high-speed cable or DSL (digital subscriber line). The dial-up access uses the telephone line to connect with the ISP. High-speed, which is increasingly available in metropolitan areas, uses cable or DSL on the telephone line. The high-speed ISPs offer broader bandwidth fast connections for the average user (commonly known as "broadband").

While a dial-up allows you to control your access connection time, the high-speed cable or DSL is continuously connected using a special modem that is provided by the ISP or purchased at a computer store. Some people have arrangements with their employers to allow them to access the company's network and Internet links over the telephone from a remote location, such as their home, and use this connection as an ISP equivalent.

Providing Information to the ISP

When you register with an ISP, you can expect to give them your name, address and telephone number. You may also have to provide a credit card number if this is your payment method. Typically, you can then assign an e-mail address and personal password to use as an authenticator when connecting with the ISP.

A Portal to Your Personal Information

Typically, your Internet browsing and e-mail travels through the Internet with little added security so that there is a risk that at any intermediary point someone could read and obtain information about you. You do not necessarily know when and where this is happening, except where you voluntarily submit your information, but can assume that this information is not fully protected.

Many Internet components, including your ISP's computers/servers, store a trail of information about your Internet access, the sites you visit and other information about you. In some cases, this trail may provide more fulsome information, such as tracking your search preferences and shopping habits or providing a means for you to tell the ISP your preferences. If your e-mail address is with your ISP, it may also have a file of the e-mails that it receives on your behalf, ready for you to download. Alternatively, you may use a specific e-mail provider, such as Hotmail or Yahoo, which also has the capability to track the searches you do on its website. Your ISP may also have back-up copies of your personal web pages and your information briefcases and storage space.

In all, your ISP has access to a great deal of information about your preferences, actions and behaviours and potentially could also have access to the associated personal, private and financial information. Recent criminal and terrorist investigations have given rise to controversy over what access can be made to this type of information without the user's consent.

The Personal Profile

Many ISPs, e-mail services and broader Internet information services, such as Yahoo and Hotmail, encourage you to retain information about yourself in a personal profile. As you can reference this information multiple times, the personal profile eliminates the need for you to input personal information.

Moderate to High Risk

Be cautious as to what information you disclose in a personal profile. As others could easily access this information, do NOT complete a personal profile where you have the option.

Other ISP Services

Increasingly ISPs offer other services such as:
- Space to maintain personal web pages (called a web space) or a website
- Virus scanning protection of e-mail
- Anti-spamming services
- News Groups, Bulletin Boards and Chat Lines, and
- Information briefcases and/or free information storage space.

ISPs provide virus scanning, anti-spamming or e-mail encryption services in order to deal with problems before they become bigger problems for both its customers and the ISP itself. However, if these services are available to you, do not rely solely on them. For example, a computer virus may come from a source other than e-mail.

PRACTICAL STEPS TO PROTECT YOURSELF
Your Internet Service Provider

- Only provide the minimal amount of personal and financial information required to sign up for the ISP service.
- Limit the amount of personal preference information you disclose in a personal profile when registering with a provider.
- Do not rely solely on any protection services, such as virus scanning, that your ISP may provide. For example, you should also install a virus scanner on your computer and keep it up-to-date as well as configure your e-mail system to detect potential spamming. See Chapter 11.

- Be continuously aware that your ISP can track your Internet activities and behaviours and may observe more of your personal and financial information than you would wish to disclose.
- Where you have a choice, do not allow the ISP to create a personal profile of your information.

ACCESSING THE INTERNET USING PDAs AND POCKET COMPUTERS

Increasingly the online capabilities of PDAs and other pocket computers (usually wireless connections) are being used to browse the web and process e-mails. All of the precautions regarding the disclosure and protection of personal information apply equally to these devices.

Moderate to High Risk

Portable computing devices present additional risks for which you need to take additional preventative measures.
- These small computing devices are more easily lost or stolen.
- Anyone who has access to your PDA can access any personal and private information you have stored there.
- The PDA can be attached to a PC to transfer files and folders from one to the other. While this is an attractive feature for your personal use, keep in mind that it also means anyone else with access to your PDA or your personal computer also can do this.

PRACTICAL STEPS TO PROTECT YOURSELF
Using PDAs and Other Small Computing Devices
- Treat your PDA or pocket computer as you would your personal computer, e.g., password-protect access to it and always power it down when not in use.
- Apply all applicable steps and principles outlined in this book to protect yourself and your PDA when online.
- Safeguard your device at all times. Do NOT leave it unattended, e.g., on your office desk.

Technical step to consider:
- Use encryption software to secure (in addition to your personal password) any personal information you would not want someone else to access when using the Internet. Encryption functions may be part of your PDA or pocket computer or you may have to purchase and install encryption software. See Chapter 15.

ACCESSING THE INTERNET FROM ANOTHER COMPUTER

When computing or sending personal, financial or private information on another computer when you are away from home, you risk disclosing more personal information than you would want others to know. You may be using public computers, such as those available at places such as school or university, public libraries, Internet cafes, airport business centres, technical trade shows and conference centres, or you may be plugging in your laptop at a hotel or other facility.

If you are using a computer at a company, be aware that many enterprises have policies against personal use of their computers and the browsing of certain websites. Indeed, their firewalls may technically prevent you from accessing certain types of websites. Consider also that the company will have trails of your activity and attempted activities that provide details about your online preferences and behaviours.

Low to High Risk

Keep in mind that:

- Companies, libraries and other places where you may use another computer are likely to have sophisticated computer technology and knowledgeable technicians. Be wary about computing sensitive personal information. A technician may want to know about your personal information, such as your salary.
- It may be fairly simple for someone to get access to the computer or the network to which it is connected and access your personal, financial and private information.
- You may not know what is installed on the computer or have the access authority to find out; e.g., someone could plant keystroke recorder software on the computer you are using and recover everything that you have input, including your identifier/name and passwords.
- In the same way that your ISP retains a trail of your electronic travels, including all the websites you visit and the e-mail stored on your behalf, the ISP for another computer may also have a similar record and trail.
- Be aware of temporary Internet files and automatic back-up applications. Be sure to delete these properly when you have finished using another computer. Temporary files are discussed in Chapters 10 and 15.

...

- If you use your laptop in a hotel room, you will likely need to dial-up to your ISP. In this case, all of your online activity will also go through the hotel's switchboard, much of it transmitted like a postcard in plain text. The risks involved when travelling are discussed in Chapter 2.
- Many hotel chains now offer wireless connectivity within their complex. Since the wireless network's radio waves are similar to those used for radio stations and cordless phones, the transmissions could be potentially intercepted by anyone with the right kind of receiver on the same bandwidth. Hotel staff or other guests in close proximity to your computer could hack into your wireless online communications without your knowledge. Wireless connections are discussed in Chapter 15.

PRACTICAL STEPS TO PROTECT YOURSELF
Personal Computing on Another Computer
- Be EXTRA cautious of what personal, financial or private information you disclose online when using another computer or your laptop when connected to another network, such as in a hotel. Determine whether you really need to do this and now, in this place and what would be the implications if someone else observed all your online activity.
- Do NOT compute personal, financial and private information while online at your workplace or school, on a public computer or on your laptop while travelling unless absolutely necessary and you know that it is safe.
- Be sure that you know what information you are leaving behind when you use another computer. This includes automatic back-ups of word processing documents, e-mail attachments saved to a temporary file and browser cache files. Review the settings and options in the software you use to locate where the information is stored, even temporarily.
- Delete files and then empty the Recycling Bin and the browser cache. Ensure that these files are deleted and not just recycled.
- Be cautious when using software or third party websites to access stored personal and financial information remotely. Log on and ensure the information is encrypted when transmitted to you. You should be able to confirm and control the encryption; that is, you should be able to set your own encryption keys.
- Always log off a website on which you have logged on.
- Always close down your browser when you have finished browsing and before someone else uses it.

- Regularly clear the cache, Internet temporary and history files, and disable AutoComplete of user names and passwords on forms on the computer you are using.

Using Your Laptop While Travelling

- When travelling with your laptop, only use a wireless network if you are able to control and configure the encryption on the link.

ANONYMITY ON THE INTERNET

Anonymity is an increasingly popular vehicle for travelling the information highway.

Moderate to High Risk

Many people use fake identifiers/names as their e-mail address. For example, you could set up the e-mail address John148246@hotmail.com or similar free e-mail service even though your given name may actually be Hyacinth Heritage. Only the ISP that operates the e-mail service may know your true identity but even this and your address could be falsified and are rarely checked.

Some software and services will proxy your actual electronic identity and create an anonymous identity each time you use the Internet to browse. However, these services have recently been under scrutiny to ensure that they are not helping terrorists and other undesirables to hide behind anonymity on the Internet. Other abuses of anonymity include persons who use it to operate in socially undesirable ways on Chat Lines and Bulletin Boards. The targets are often children, the elderly or other dependent, vulnerable persons. They build their victim's trust online and then abuse it. Some have lured children to secret meetings with tragic consequences.

While anonymity can help you to maintain the secret of your identity and privacy, in today's increasingly complex world, there are moves to curtail its use due to terrorism, stalkers and the other criminal activities it affords.

...

Digital certificates are a tool that helps authenticate and identify people electronically and enable them to digitally sign information. They can also be used to achieve anonymity. The authority that issues the digital certificate does not need to include the user's real name in the certificate, but rather could use an identifier that only they can link to the true owner. This is advanced technology, but operates today in some international financial institutions. Digital certificates are discussed in Chapter 14.

PRACTICAL STEPS TO PROTECT YOURSELF
Anonymity on the Internet

- Keep in mind that if you can create a fictitious name/identifier and use a physical address to which you have no connection, so can other people. Be cautious.
- If you do use software or a service to create an anonymous identity when you browse the Internet, give the service provider factual information about yourself so that your activities are not under suspicion.

COMMUNICATING
ON THE INTERNET

13

Where you are simply searching for information on the Internet, it is generally a low-risk activity. However, if you can find information about others on the Internet, others can likely find the same information about you. If you do not want this information to be shared, find out how to remove your personal data from these services, in the same way that you might choose to have an unlisted telephone number. Where you do not have to disclose certain information, take advantage of this option.

Many websites offer simple directories for looking up the name and address of a person or business and finding the telephone number. Sometimes you may be asked to input personal information before your enquiry is processed. While you may only be asked for a phone number or your e-mail address, be aware that this information could be used for telemarketing or spam mail.

E-MAIL

E-mail (or electronic mail) is likely the most often used vehicle on the information highway. Using widely available e-mail software, users are able to communicate to anyone who has an e-mail address, anywhere in the world. You can include links to websites in an e-mail as well as attachments, such as files with information, pictures, music or software.

E-mail gives everyone the ability to exchange and share information widely and quickly... but not necessarily confidentially. E-mail can be read by anyone because you do not know how many intermediates or servers the e-mail passes through and where its content may be stored and retained.

When deciding whether you should communicate certain information in an e-mail, the simple test is: Would you send this sensitive information on a postcard in the regular postal service to this person or organization? Would you expect the recipient to reply on a postcard?

Securing E-mail

Few ISPs offer or provide encryption or even personal e-mail encryption services that scramble your information. However, there are software solutions that address the concern that your ISP and/or other unknown parties could capture the information you are requesting and/or sending and store it for analysis by their computers.

Some of the software solutions include providing privacy by encryption and authentication by digital signatures. Digital signatures are further discussed in Chapter 14; encryption is discussed in Chapter 15. These capabilities are included in some standard consumer software, while others are plug-ins or add-ons. Examples include S/MIME (Secure Multipurpose Internet Mail Extensions), PGP (Pretty Good Privacy) and PEM (Privacy Enhance Mail).

To secure your e-mail, both the sender of the e-mail and the recipient must have compatible e-mail security software that encrypts the message and any attachments. This security software allows you to create your own secret key that you provide to those people who will receive the secure e-mail from you. Entering the key allows the recipient to open and read the e-mail.

As intermediary parties who may intercept your e-mail will not have your secret key, the e-mail and the attachments cannot be read or altered by others. When the recipients receive the secure e-mail, they must correctly enter the secret key that you have provided to them. If the e-mail and attachment successfully decrypt and the signature is validated as correct, the recipient has good assurance that the e-mail came from you and has not been read or altered by anyone else.

The use of encryption and digital signatures is increasingly commonplace in business to secure e-mail within an enterprise and e-mail between its customers and suppliers. However for the average consumer, this is not yet a mature area. You will need to research and do some trial and error with recipients to ensure that your e-mail security features are working.

Low to High Risk

If you use the Internet to send e-mail that includes family stories, comments on the weather and other like topics and occasionally attach a picture or a joke, you are a low-risk user. However, if you use e-mail to communicate with your financial services institution about your finances and investments or to provide sensitive information such as checking your credit record, your risk would range from moderate to high, depending on the precautions you take.

PRACTICAL STEPS TO PROTECT YOURSELF
Using E-mail
- Treat your e-mail like a postcard that can be read by anyone.
- Do NOT send e-mails containing sensitive personal, financial or private information unless you secure them by using encryption.
- Where you believe you would benefit from secure e-mail, ask your ISP to provide this feature.

Technical step to consider:
- Acquire and install a secure e-mail solution, such as PGP (Pretty Good Privacy). Create and distribute your secret key to others who use compatible software with whom you want to exchange secure e-mail. Do not send the key by e-mail.

PRIVACY LAWS AND POLICY
Virtually every website you visit today has a privacy button that lets you access the organization's privacy policy. In Canada, privacy and the use of electronic information are now subject to an Act of Parliament, the *Personal Information Protection and Electronic Documents Act 2000* (PIPEDA). Enterprises are required to comply with principles that are intended to protect the consumer.

The federal PIPEDA supports and promotes electronic commerce by providing:
- Guidelines for the use of electronic means to communicate or record information, and
- Rules to govern the collection, use and disclosure of personal information in the course of commercial activity.

The principles of the PIPEDA are intended to govern privacy for all websites (including cross border websites) by requiring that the privacy practices and policies are disclosed and the enterprise is in compliance and accountable for privacy matters.

Generally enterprises must:
- Identify the purpose for the collection of information
- Obtain consent to collect, share and disclose information
- Limit collection, use, disclosure and retention
- Ensure accuracy, quality and correctness of data and information
- Provide safeguards and security protection over private and personal information
- Maintain openness in the development of privacy procedures and policies
- Provide individuals with access to obtain and review information retained on them

- Provide recourse for individuals for breaches of privacy and the ability to challenge any incorrect and/or out-of-date information, and
- Be accountable for privacy matters within the enterprise.

Most privacy policies will include statements about each of these principles. In this way, you have some assurance of the enterprise's compliance even if you are using a non-Canadian website. However, some privacy policies are clearly more focused towards legal concerns and read like the small print of hard copy consumer agreements. Recently the media reported that many online enterprises created a false sense of trust by having a good privacy policy, but were found not to be following it.

P3P Privacy Protocol

To overcome inconsistencies in privacy practices, a North American privacy protocol, P3P, has been developed. P3P is intended to enforce a consistent process for enterprises to categorize their website as to the level of compliance with the principles. The newer versions of browsers, such as Microsoft Internet Explorer 6.0, will read this information and warn you if the level does not meet your specified acceptable level. This approach is in the early stages of adoption and will need broad acceptance by enterprises and governments if it is to be meaningful.

ENROLLING ON A WEBSITE

Many enterprises that you may have enrolled with, such as the websites of a hotel or car rental company, may ask you for basic personal information relevant to the service they offer. This information may include your name, address and phone number, credit card information and membership number for air mile rewards. While you may want to take advantage of member benefits such as faster check-in/check-out and special discounts, you need to be sure that these benefits do not entail risks to your identity and privacy.

These enterprises often want to ensure that the information they gather about you is current and correct as well as have you agree to revised terms and conditions to the service and send you the revised privacy policy. You should take this opportunity to check your record and correct anything that is out-of-date. Also take time to read the small print of the terms and conditions and privacy policy; however, be aware that these can be very long legal-like documents. One website has a service agreement that is 59 pages long!

When enrolling on some websites, you may be given options about whether you must provide certain personal information. This option may simply be presented in the form of a request as to whether you would like to be sent e-mails notifying you about products and special offers. This is an important opportunity for you to control your choices and ensure that your information, including your e-mail address, is only used for purposes to which you agree.

Confirmations

A best practice when enrolling at a website (or completing an online form as discussed below) is that the enterprise will send to you an e-mail to confirm your registration and any changes that you subsequently make. For example, if you amend your e-mail address when reviewing your profile, the enterprise may e-mail you at your new address to confirm the change. This practice provides some assurance that you made the change and no one has ambushed your identity and password to make the changes.

Completing Online Forms

Some websites may have online forms to send/give information to the enterprise or apply for a product or service. For example, you may apply for an insurance product through an insurer's website or for a service or grant through a government website. Websites that provide forms for customers to complete online are usually designated as secure websites. If they are not, the information you send could be accessed and read as easily as one would read an e-mail or postcard.

Secure web sites are recognized with HTTPS before the site address instead of HTTP. The HTTPS indicates that the site is secured by SSL (Secure Sockets Layer). Depending on your browser, you may also see a closed padlock or key icon displayed that indicates the use of SSL. SSL is discussed in Chapter 14.

Tax Preparation Services

Increasingly it is possible to prepare and submit your income tax return to the CCRA using a web-based service. This online form filling approach allows you to enter all your tax slips and deductions, calculate your balance and submit your tax return for processing. Many services allow you to save some of your work and come back to the site and complete it later. Most services charge a fee for doing this.

As a minimum, these web-based services should be secure by SSL and should provide you with the protection of an ID and the selection of your own personal password.

Moderate to High Risk

Most of the Internet activity described in this section could be considered as a moderate risk, particularly if you are dealing with the websites of known and reputable organizations and institutions. Knowing the company with which you are dealing and being satisfied with its quality and reputation are the best ways to protect yourself.

However, be aware that many websites are start-up companies. Surveys have found that many of them may not be careful about complying with privacy protocols. Only provide the required personal and financial information at reputable websites, such as those of your financial services institution, government and known merchants, where you have greater comfort that the intended security is operating effectively and that the privacy policy is enforced. The security afforded by the Secure Sockets Layer, SSL, found on some websites is discussed in Chapter 14.

Beyond our Canadian borders, your information may not be subject to Canadian laws and rules. You need to be cautious about providing information to enterprises located outside of Canada since you do not know the privacy regulations and how this information is handled or may be used.

PRACTICAL STEPS TO PROTECT YOURSELF
Disclosing and Obtaining Information Online

- Be cautious about what personal, financial or private information you disclose when giving information over the Internet.
- Only provide personal or financial information at websites of reputable, known organizations.
- Only rely on the security practices (i.e., SSL or more advanced security) of your financial services institution, government sites and well-known reputable companies and service providers. Be wary about providing personal or tax information at other websites.

LOGGING ON AND OFF WEBSITES

For purposes of this discussion, the terms log on, log off also include log in, log out, sign in, sign out, and enter and exit. When you log on to a website, you identify yourself to a computer to which you have connected over the Internet. During the procedure, you are usually asked to input your user name and password.

To terminate a session, you must specifically log off to prevent other users continuing your session. The session should be completed and closed properly every time by specifically logging out of the site. When a website requires you to log on and enter your identification/name and password (e.g., to access your online banking, get web-based e-mail or enter the members' area of a vendor's website), it should also have a log out or equivalent button so you can terminate your session.

If you do not log off, your session may remain active. Although some websites may have a time-out feature that automatically logs you off if you are inactive at the website, you cannot count on this for protecting your money, privacy and identity as you do not know how long your session may remain active. Do not take chances. Always log off.

Low to High Risk

Always log off after you have completed your session at a log on website, such as at the website of your financial services institution or web-based e-mail. If you do not terminate the session properly, someone could take it over to perform actions as if you were still online, e.g., access your financial accounts.

Always close down the browser software when you have finished a session. When you close the browser software, you prevent the next user from simply clicking on the back button in the browser to reload your pages from cache and potentially read your financial statement, investment records or other sensitive information you may have just used.

If you are not going to use your computer for some time, either close it down or ensure that it automatically goes into sleep or hibernation mode. Screen saver, sleep and hibernation modes are discussed in Chapter 10. This protection step is particularly important where your computer is continuously connected to the Internet, i.e. by cable or DSL (high speed).

PRACTICAL STEPS TO PROTECT YOURSELF
Browsing on the Internet
- Always log off a website when you finish your session.
- Always close down your browser when you have finished browsing and before someone else uses it.

- Always shut down your computer or ensure it is deactivated and password-protected by the screen saver, sleep or hibernation mode when your computer is not in use for an extended period of time.
- If a pop-up screen offers a free download of software, close it. The software may contain "spyware". Spyware is discussed in Chapter 11.

Using Different Passwords for Different Risks

One of the techniques to help you remember all of your passwords and passphrases (but NOT your banking PINs) is to consider grouping their use with the different types of risks you accept. For example, you could use the same password for several websites that you regularly use to make it easier to remember it. Of course, you need to ensure the risk is similar for each website as well as regularly change your password or passphrase (at least every three months), for example, where you subscribe to bill presentment from several utilities, or subscribe to multiple news services.

If you buy items or services from a number of websites, you should have a different and longer passwords or passphrases to log on at each of these websites. You should change the password once a month due to the increased risk.

Low to High Risk

Where the risk is low, consider using the same password for logging on at similar websites. However, do not use the same password to log on at websites where you use a credit card to buy items online. Someone who discovers your password for the one website could access all the other services for which you use the same password.

PRACTICAL STEPS TO PROTECT YOURSELF
Protecting Your Electronic Identity

- Use different passwords for different levels of risk.
- Consider using the same password or passphrase for web services that are at the same low level of risk, e.g., utility bill presentment services.
- Change your passwords regularly.
- Do NOT use the same PINs or passwords for online banking and brokerage transactions. These should always be unique for each service.

A PERSONAL WEBSITE

Most commercial ISPs and many other services such as Yahoo offer personal web space for you to create and store a website that they will host for you. Providing this service builds customer loyalty and increases usage. You may also decide to create and register your own domain name, such as www.john.smith.com or www.john.smith.name. Other domain extensions, such as .org, .net, and .ca, are also available.

Many people use a personal web space or registered website as an opportunity to create simple information pages about their hobbies, family, cars or pets, while others create complex family trees dating back hundreds of years. These websites provide a wealth of valuable personal information and preferences for visitors, including criminals. Many of these sites proudly post names, addresses, dates and places of birth, age, the mother's maiden names, the spouse's name, children's names, pet's names and information such as where and when a couple married, along with photographs.

While these personal websites may be good fun, they can have serious unintended consequences. All of this posted information could be used to hack your passwords or even steal your identity. The information could also be used to do personal business in your name, such as apply for a driving licence or financial account or take out a loan.

If you decide to have a personal website, be sure to post only limited and general personal information, such as "born in 1953". You should also search your name periodically on various search engines, such as Google, to see whether someone else has posted the family history or genealogical chart and disclosed valuable personal information about you and your family.

Storing Information on a Website

Sometimes users store important information on websites or web spaces provided by an ISP or web-based services. The convenience of being able to store an extra copy of a file on a website that you can access from anywhere is appealing for people who suddenly need a back-up copy, such as a presenter using a PowerPoint file. Besides being useful in an emergency, the website access to files is helpful if you want to make information available to others, such as giving participants access to your slides after a presentation.

However, others could access all of the information that you store on your website or web space. At a minimum, the employees of the ISP or web service provider could access this information. For this reason, information you store on your web space or website, including sensitive information, is not secure and could be easily read or copied and even changed. Be selective as to what type of information you store on a website or web space. Alternatively, ensure the information is encrypted and password protected.

Posting Resumés

If you use a website (or Bulletin Board or Chat Line) to post or distribute your resumé, provide the minimum of personal information that will allow people to assess your experience and qualifications and know how to contact you. A telephone number and e-mail address are usually sufficient. Do not include sensitive personal information, such as your home address, your date of birth or social insurance number.

Low to High Risk

Creating personal websites, storing information on a website and posting resumés are activities where the risk could range from low to high depending on your activities and the precautions you take.

PRACTICAL STEPS TO PROTECT YOURSELF
Posting and Storing Information on Websites

- Do NOT disclose personal, financial and private information on a personal web space or website or through posting your resumé on the Internet.
- If posting your resumé on a website, provide only the minimum personal information needed to assess your experience and qualifications and to contact you, i.e., telephone number and e-mail address. Do NOT include your home address, your date of birth, social insurance number or other sensitive personal information.
- Do NOT use website facilities to store full system back-ups because there is a risk that additional programs could be added to your programs, including viruses and Trojan horses.

Technical step to consider:

- If you must store personal, private or financial information on a website for remote access, ensure the information is encrypted and password protected.

CUSTOMIZED HOME PAGES

Many people who browse or surf the Internet create a customized page within their browser, typically known as a "home" page, so that the opening screen greets them with their selections of daily information. These might include the latest news, sports scores, business information, stock quotes, the weather forecast, a daily horoscope, gambling odds, and in some services, important reminders such as birthdays and anniversaries.

When you set up a customized page such as "MyServices", you are specifically choosing services and are often asked to provide detailed information. You may also be asked to specify your preference for further services, such as if you like to play golf, whether you would like information about golf holidays. All of this information about you is retained and stored by the service that provides the customized home page. You may be asked to check it or update it periodically.

Always be very careful about what information you give. Keep it to an absolute minimum and regularly check what information is being kept about you. If you are not sure why the information is being requested, ask. If you do not receive a reasonable response (better than "because we need it"), do not provide the information.

Low Risk

Generally, the customized home page is a low-risk activity. However, your assessment depends on the nature of the personal, financial or private information that you choose to disclose to the provider. Remember the customized home page is an optional service and the information you provide is voluntary.

PRACTICAL STEPS TO PROTECT YOURSELF
Using Customized Home Pages
- Be cautious about what personal, financial or private information you disclose when registering and using customized home pages and online services such as "MyServices".

News Groups, Bulletin Boards and Chat Lines

Most ISPs provide access to News Groups or Bulletin Boards on specific areas of interest, and Chat Lines for more instant communications and discussions than e-mail provides. These forums cover a broad range of topics and opinions and most of the discussion is conducted anonymously.

Simply put, assume that everyone you are dealing with in these forums is a stranger. Do not disclose sensitive personal, financial or private information; that is, keep in mind the difference between comments or opinions that you would like to share and personal facts about you and your family that you should not share with a stranger. Even if you feel that there is a good reason for disclosing the information and you do so voluntarily and in an informed manner, why do it over the Internet to a Chat Line where others can intercept this information? These forums are a good source for criminals to obtain information about your identity as well as your e-mail IP address in order to perpetrate their schemes.

Low to High Risk

If you are a cautious and infrequent user of News Groups, Bulletin Boards and Chat Lines, your risk is low. However, if you use these services regularly and consistently and disclose personal identifying information, your risk may be moderate or even high.

PRACTICAL STEPS TO PROTECT YOURSELF
News Groups, Bulletin Boards and Chat Lines
- Do NOT disclose personal, financial and private information in these forums.

Technical step to consider:
- Install a firewall so that your IP address cannot be identified and attacked when accessing News Groups, Bulletin Boards and Chat Lines. See Chapter 15.

FILE-SHARING SERVICES

Sharing files over the Internet is an increasingly popular activity and not just amongst teenagers. The files are most often music, although services are increasingly offering pictures, graphics, and video files. Napster was one of the earliest websites offering these Internet tools for finding and downloading MP3 music files. Other websites offer similar services.

In most instances, you simply do not know:
- How safe the sharing software is.
- Who you are sharing files with online (most users are anonymous).
- What else these files may be capable of doing on your computer.

To use file-sharing services, you must download the software that connects you to other users of the system and then let it search the Internet for the artist or title of music that you wish to share and copy. The software should be automatically configured to only share files from specific controlled folders on every user's computer. However, many of these file-sharing services do not let you specify the folder for sharing. If the artist or title is found, the search results presented to you include all the files that people are prepared to share. You then select the file you want to copy. Note that you should only see the files in the folders assigned to the software that the other person wants to share. The file is then downloaded to your computer by the software and stored in the folder that you have designated as your sharing folder. Others may then copy it from your shared folder. You can move it or copy it to a music folder and then play it.

While most sharing software is only intended to work with the shared folders, you do not know with certainty that this is always the case. For this reason, you need to take some additional precautions to ensure that no one can break out of the software and search your computer for other files, including your personal, financial and private information.

High Risk

Using file-sharing software is very different from sharing files across internal networks, a LAN, and in your home. Sharing files from freely available software across the Internet is generally a high-risk activity.

Simply put, do not use the file-sharing vehicle online unless you know what you are doing, take measures to secure your personal, financial and private information, and ensure that files are not inadvertently shared with others. Essentially, these services allow files to be downloaded from another computer (including yours) that has the sharing software. Keep in mind that if you are using Napster-type services, you could be providing MP3 files to the world. File-sharing services can also be the source of unwanted and unseen spyware and viruses on your computer.

Remember that the website can be physically anywhere in the world. There are also copyright laws and related issues to consider. If you do participate in this activity, consider the technical steps below. Also see Chapter 15 for a discussion of firewall protection.

PRACTICAL STEPS TO PROTECT YOURSELF
Using File-sharing Software

• Avoid using file-sharing software on the Internet.

Technical steps to consider:

If you use file-sharing software on the Internet:

• Ensure that the sharing capability provided by your computer's operating system is only activated on a restricted number of your folders, if any at all.

Typically this feature is only needed where you are part of a network (LAN or WLAN) and you want to share specific files, folders or programs. For example, in Windows 2000, you can find the option to share by right clicking on a folder name. In Windows Explorer, the shared folder is shown as being held by an open hand.

- Install personal firewall software on your computer in addition to any hardware firewall. The software firewall should be configured to detect and prevent anyone trying to access folders that you do not want to share. Firewalls are discussed in Chapter 15.
- Create a separate partition on the hard drive or install a separate hard drive in your computer for using file-sharing software. This will prevent anyone from searching other information that is stored on the other hard drive or partition in your computer.

14

PROTECTING YOUR
ONLINE TRANSACTIONS

The volume and risk of online transactions are continuously increasing; some observers suggest exponentially. From buying goods and services, accessing financial accounts, eliminating paper bills, bidding at auctions to participating in online gambling, each activity has a different inherent risk. The risk is further affected by the reputation of the website or merchant with which you are doing business or whether you know the person with whom you are trading.

This chapter discusses many of the increasingly common online transaction processes and outlines the security protection you can expect to be in place to protect your transactions, including encryption and digital signatures.

BUYING ONLINE

The ability to buy goods and services online is another benefit of the Internet that many people now use regularly and safely. The most popular items purchased at websites are books, CDs and DVDs, event tickets, software programs and larger items such as computers. Some website providers will deliver flowers or gifts across the country and to recipients in other countries. Increasingly, auction sites offer a wide range of new, used or memorabilia items for purchase by, and from, individuals and enterprises.

Membership Programs

Company websites that offer membership programs want you to be satisfied with your shopping experience and come back many times. When asked to enroll, make sure you understand why the company requires the information being requested and decide what information you want to give.

The ability to decide what personal information you provide is an important issue. The website may simply give you the option as to whether you would like to be sent e-mails about its products and special offers. If the website allows you to choose not to receive marketing e-mails, this is an important opportunity for you to control your choices and ensure that your information, including your e-mail address, is not used for purposes to which you have not agreed.

Typically when you enroll at one of these websites, you will be assigned or asked to choose an identifier/name and to select a personal password in order to access the members' section of the site where you can take advantage of special offers or frequent user privileges. Many sites simplify this process by making your e-mail address your identifier.

When you make a purchase, the process is generally simpler if you are a member, although you need to provide your identifier/name and password. With your information registered, this means you only to confirm information such as the delivery address rather than input it each time you make a purchase. This can be particularly useful if you are bidding on an item in an auction or trying to buy very popular event tickets that will quickly sell out. You should only need to enter your payment preference, e.g., your credit card information, to complete the purchase, and then wait for the merchandise/tickets to arrive.

Always save or print the purchase confirmation page as a record of the transaction. As this will usually have a confirmation number, it will be useful if you need to track the delivery of the purchase or to pick up event tickets at a box office.

Low to High Risk

When you make purchases on the Internet, your risk moves from the low risk of giving information about yourself that relates to your identity, to the higher risk of giving information that relates to your finances and paying for goods and services online.

Avoid using websites that store your credit card number and its expiry date when you make purchases. If storing the credit card information is not optional, do not make purchases at that website. Even though these websites may keep your credit card information continuously safe, it is safer and simpler to re-enter your current or preferred credit card number each time you make an online purchase.

Some online purchasing may be in association with your online banking service and allow you to make your payment in the same way you pay a utility bill. Your risk here is low; however, your risk rises to moderate when you use a credit card to make your purchase. Another form of payment may be a high risk.

Generally, reputable websites operated by well-known companies, governments and financial services institutions provide greater assurance that the intended security is operating effectively and that the company's privacy policy is enforced. Security at websites is discussed below.

PRACTICAL STEPS TO PROTECT YOURSELF
Buying Goods and Services Online

- Be cautious of what personal, financial or private information you disclose when buying merchandise or services on a website, particularly when using an auction site or trading with an individual.
- Only disclose personal or financial information on websites of organizations that you consider to be reputable.
- Avoid using websites that store and retain your credit card number and expiry date.
- Rely on the security practices (i.e., SSL or more advanced security) of only your financial service institution, government sites and reputable merchants and service providers.

SSL — SECURE SOCKETS LAYER

Websites that ask for and collect information using form completion or payment capabilities are usually designated as secure websites. Secure websites are recognized by HTTPS before the site address instead of the more familiar HTTP.

HTTPS indicates that the website is secured by SSL (Secure Sockets Layer). Your browser may also display a graphic of a closed lock or a solid key to indicate this security measure is in place at a website.

SSL encrypts the information between your computer and the website's server using keys provided by the enterprise's server. The encryption scrambles the information you are sending so that no one else can read it. Even if an intermediary on the Internet stored it, it would be encrypted and unreadable.

How do you know SSL is safe? Simply put, you do not know. The SSL technology secures the information you send to and from the server or to the gateway inside the firewall that supports the website. Your information is therefore encrypted to that server. Beyond that server, however, the information may be processed by another computer application and may not be encrypted inside the firewall. Additionally, your information may be stored on the server temporarily or longer and could be accessible to the enterprise's employees, agents of the web service and even hackers.

If SSL is not properly and continuously configured at the receiving server to encrypt all information from browsers, the information you transmit may be as transparent as a postcard. In fact, you could get a false positive indication (e.g., the lock or key is displayed on your browser) to indicate a secure session, but your information may be sent as transparently as a postcard.

Recent versions of browsers have the ability to confirm the security features of a website, e.g., the encryption algorithm being used and the length of the key (this should be at least 128 bits). Check as to whether your browser confirms SSL is in place. If it does not confirm this, consider upgrading to a new version of the browser.

Generally, the issue of security centres on the reputation of the website you are using. If you only disclose personal, financial and private information at reputable, secured websites, such as those of your financial services provider, the government and reputable vendors, you have reasonable assurance that the SSL is operating effectively.

Internet communications to a website that does not use SSL are NOT secure unless you explicitly know that the website is using another security software or you have downloaded and installed security software or a browser plug-in solution on your computer.

PRACTICAL STEPS TO PROTECT YOURSELF
Ensuring Websites are Secure
- Before disclosing sensitive personal and financial information, ensure the website is reputable.
- Rely on the security practices (i.e., SSL or more advanced security) of only your financial services institution, government sites and reputable merchants. The HTTPS in the address indicates that the website is secured by SSL.

ONLINE FINANCIAL SERVICES
Many people are reluctant to use the Internet to access their financial information and money online. This reluctance stems from being used to doing their banking at bricks and mortar branches, dealing with people face to face, and having the security of cameras or security guards. Regardless, financial services online do have benefits other than the convenience of not having to line up at a teller or ABM. With online financial services, you can manage your accounts when and where you want, as well as effectively manage the access to your accounts.

Online banking systems allow you to see almost immediately that your transaction has cleared your financial account. For example, if your spouse or partner is out shopping and you happen to be online, the direct debit point-of-sale transactions will likely appear online as they happen. Therefore, if any transactions appear that you or your spouse or partner did not authorize, particularly on your credit card accounts, you can contact your financial services institution immediately before more unauthorized transactions take place. They can review them with you immediately and potentially suspend your account or credit card before more transactions take place. Quick action will reduce the extent of your losses from fraudulent transactions.

Linking Accounts to these Services

Many online systems allow you to change the relationship between your services and the accounts you have. Many people have more than one account and may also use several services, such as ABMs, telephone banking and online banking to access their accounts and complete transactions. Some online banking services allow you to change the accounts you want to have access to at each of these services. For example, you may routinely access your chequing account for certain transactions but have some money set aside in a daily interest savings account earning some interest. You may not want the savings account accessible from all services in case you lose your electronic identity, e.g., your bankcard and PIN. In this way, the thief would have fewer accounts from which to withdraw your money.

A good precaution when travelling abroad is to have only one account linked to your bankcard with just enough funds for the period you are away. If you do use an unsafe ABM while on vacation, this precaution will reduce the amount of losses that could occur through fraudulent transactions.

Some online banking offers other services beyond banking and investments, for example utility bill presentment and payment, purchases of goods and services, and the purchase of travel insurance and other products and services. These can be accessed and used voluntarily at your convenience using the financial services institution's security protection.

PRACTICAL STEPS TO PROTECT YOURSELF
Using Online Financial Services

- Use your online service to monitor your balances and recent transactions.
- Use your online service to manage the relationships and access between your services and accounts, such as your bankcard and telephone banking. Consider restricting access to your savings account, i.e., do not have it accessible through telephone or online banking.

THIRD PARTY TRANSFERS OR E-MAIL TRANSFERS

The transfer of money to a third party using an online service and e-mail is gaining popularity. These online/e-mail transfer services can be used to make payments for amounts owed or to transfer funds to family members in an emergency, such as to a student who is away at university.

Where provided by your financial services provider, these services are usually part of your online banking service and are often referred to as e-mail transfers. Some services require you to select and use a separate password to access this e-mail transfer service. This requires filling out an online form, indicating the amount you want to send, the account from which the funds are to be withdrawn, and the e-mail address of the receiving party. The transfer can be completed without your knowing the banking information of the receiving party.

Additionally, you may need to use a specific password identifier for the transfer. For example, you may provide a question and the answer that the recipient must successfully provide to complete the transfer. When you send the transfer from your online banking, it may be withdrawn from your account immediately. The receiving party receives an e-mail notification that the money is available (but not how much), and where to go on the web to claim it. When giving the recipient the answer to the secret question, it is best to do this by telephone. Keep in mind that e-mail is as transparent as a postcard and may not be private.

On accessing the website to claim the transfer, the recipients may be able to select their own online banking service and log on to that website as they would do for online banking. There will likely be a message to inform them that they have a transfer to claim and the option as to which account the deposit is to be transferred. When they have successfully answered the question or provided the password you set up, the funds are deposited into their account for immediate use. Some services will arrange the transfer directly if the receiver does not have an online service, but there may be an additional service fee.

The e-mail to the recipient of the transfer may indicate that the transfer will expire if not claimed within a specific number of days, such as 30 days. If the funds are not claimed, the financial institution sends an e-mail notification to the originator that the transfer can be reclaimed.

Where the service is provided in conjunction with your financial institution, the transfer limits may occasionally change. It may be a limit per transfer, a daily limit or a monthly transfer limit.

Ask if you can decline this service or set lower transfer limits for your use. Being able to decline the service will reduce your risk of someone hijacking your identity and transferring funds out of your accounts.

Low to Moderate Risk

Third party transfers are an attractive service for criminal activity. If you are not able to set or reduce your transfer limits or decline the third party transfer service altogether, your risk is moderate.

If you do not want to take this risk, you should explicitly instruct your financial institution that you do not want this transfer service available to you online. A few financial institutions appear to let you decline the service; however, be aware that while you need to explicitly accept the terms and conditions of the service, the financial institution may not let you turn the service off such that it can never be used.

Other online electronic payment processes are offered commercially and not linked to your financial institution accounts. Some require that you deposit money with them and provide personal information and then use e-mail and shared secrets (password identifiers) to spend or transfer the money. With these services, you are able to limit your risk in that you choose how much to send them and control your balance. If you are dealing with a non-Canadian service, find out how you can reclaim funds that you have deposited if the transfer is not completed. Also, ask whether the funds are insured against loss in the same way as your Canadian financial account is protected.

PRACTICAL STEPS TO PROTECT YOURSELF
Third Party E-mail Transfers

- Use only reputable e-mail transfer services, such as those offered by your financial services institution.
- If you never intend to use these services, decline this option and ask that it be turned off.
- Be cautious when using commercially offered payment services online. Ensure you have control of your money and can get it back if the transfer is not completed.

Bill presentment

Bill presentment of regular bills (e.g., utilities) means that there is no paper mail to be lost or intercepted and no paper toxic waste to dispose of unless you print your electronic bill. Paying the electronic bill online is cheaper and quicker than doing it at your financial services branch.

Companies offer this service in various ways:
- You collect the information at their website.
- The company e-mails an electronic bill to you.
- The company has the bill presented to you through your online banking service so that when you sign on, you collect your electronic bills.
- The company uses a service such as Canada Post's ePost to send you an e-mail notification that there is an electronic bill to be presented. You simply go the ePost website to retrieve and pay it. If you do not pick up the bill within a certain time period, it is sent to you by Canada Post mail.

Payment methods also vary. The model that presents the bill on your online banking service makes payment straightforward. Typically, you simply choose the bill to pay, the account to pay from, the amount and the payment date. Although the financial services website will even keep a record for you, you should print and file a copy of the payment confirmation information. Other services allow you to pay by credit card. Find out if the transaction is treated as an immediate cash transfer or as a transaction on the due date.

Low Risk

Generally, bill presentment is a low-risk activity over the Internet and one that you may find very convenient. You need to specify the option of bill presentment with the utility or service. A best practice is for the enterprise to send you a written confirmation by regular mail acknowledging that you have registered for electronic bill presentment.

PRACTICAL STEPS TO PROTECT YOURSELF
Bill Presentment
- Use the bill presentment services only through the websites of reputable merchants and service providers, e.g., your telephone company.
- Only rely on the security practices (i.e., SSL or more advanced security) of your financial services institution, government sites and reputable merchants and service providers.

ACCOUNT AGGREGATION

Many financial institutions offer a service referred to as account aggregation. Account aggregation involves giving a financial services company the authority to go to all your other financial services providers and collect account balances and/or statement information, and to present them collectively to you online. This service seems to be more popular in the U.S. than in Canada. One theory is that many Canadians tend to use only one financial services institution and therefore do not require this service.

Before enrolling in such a service, consider how much time this is likely to save you and whether this potential convenience is worth the trade-off to your giving up your electronic identifiers/name and personal financial information.

Enrolling for account aggregation may require:
- Signing an affidavit holding your financial services company harmless from any misuse of your electronic identity — your electronic identifier/name and associated password, and
- Providing all your electronic identifiers/name and their associated passwords to your financial services institution.

Consider also that your financial services institution will be able to analyze your accounts and may try to sell you additional services.

High Risk

Account aggregation requires that your financial services provider will need to continuously safely store and retain all of your electronic identifiers/name and passwords within their system, and to secure these from their own employees and systems. Therefore, account aggregation is often considered a high-risk activity over the Internet. It is a service that you should fully understand and carefully consider before you enroll.

An alternative to account aggregation services is to keep your financial records in a software package on your computer and individually download transaction and statement information and consolidate these records yourself. This process may take more time, but you will remain in control of your money, privacy and identity.

PRACTICAL STEPS TO PROTECT YOURSELF
Account Aggregation
- Carefully review and make sure you understand the way in which the financial services provider's account aggregation services work and are protected.
- Do NOT give your financial services provider your identity and passwords for accessing your financial records or transactions at other providers.

DIGITAL AND ELECTRONIC SIGNATURES

Many countries have enacted legislation to allow digital and electronic signatures as an alternative to traditional "pen and ink" written signatures to support online transactions. Digital and electronic signatures allow you to sign electronic information, including, for example, files, documents or e-mail. They use algorithms similar to encryption algorithms and keys/passwords to arithmetically combine the information to be signed with the electronic identity of the person signing the information.

Additionally, they can add into the arithmetic calculation other information about the data and signing process, for example, the date and time it was created or signed. Digital and electronic signatures are an enabler of paperless business and e-commerce. They are particularly useful online where trading partners may not even know each other.

Digital Signatures

Generally, a digital signature is generated using an electronic identity based on a digital certificate. Digital certificates appear to the user as large random numbers with the name of the issuing Certification Authority attached. They are issued by Certification Authorities, e.g., a financial services institution or the digital signature company VeriSign, that are designed to be highly secure facilities. The person wanting to verify the digital signature of specific information can refer to the issuing Certification Authority to determine whether the digital certificate is authentic and valid and therefore confirm the identity of the signer is valid. The Certification Authority thus has some responsibility as an independent party to protect the process.

Electronic Signatures

Generally, an electronic signature is formulated using something other than a digital certificate, for example, an electronic identifier/name and associated password or PIN. Unlike the digital signature, there may not be an issuing authority to validate the identity of the signer. For this reason, the safety of the electronic identifier/name and password is often more difficult to maintain and prove. Electronic signatures provide less assurance of the identity of the person who signed the information.

PRACTICAL STEPS TO PROTECT YOURSELF
Using Digital Signatures and Electronic Signatures
- Become familiar with the use of electronic and digital signatures and be aware of when you are required to use them.
- When using electronic confirmation of your signature, determine your liability.

GAMBLING ONLINE

Simply put, do not gamble your money and privacy on the Internet. You do not know with whom you are playing and the fairness of the software they use. Online gambling differs from casino gambling in that it is unregulated, unsupervised and not subject to inspections. The website may not even be operating in North America. Online gambling is a blind alley on the Internet and fraught with danger.

If you gamble on the Internet, you need to be aware of the risk you may be taking and ensure that you continuously protect your identity and privacy and only risk the money you intend to. Online gambling often requires that you disclose information about your identity and your finances.

Even if you are able to gamble anonymously, you will still need to pay for your stakes and receive any monetary winnings. Therefore, you will need to disclose some information about yourself, if only your name and credit card details. Unfortunately, some online gambling websites may not be reputable and may even require that you download some code to play their games. As you do not really know what this code does, this presents another risk of intrusion.

High Risk
Online gambling is generally a high-risk activity. If you gamble online, protect your identity and privacy by implementing the high-risk security protections outlined in Chapter 9 and discussed throughout these chapters.

PRACTICAL STEPS TO PROTECT YOURSELF
Gambling Online
- Do NOT gamble online.

AutoComplete

Internet Explorer includes a feature known as AutoComplete that completes your inputting even after you input just one letter. The feature is intended to assist you in that you do not have to re-enter your user name (ID) and password on web pages from various sites.

However, this feature also allows anyone using your computer to automatically log on under your identity without having to know your identifier and password, including your online banking and brokerage services. You should disable certain features of AutoComplete and be aware of it when using a public computer.

The functions available to help you disable AutoComplete vary between browser software and versions. Use the browser Help function to find instructions on how to disable AutoComplete.

PRACTICAL STEPS TO PROTECT YOURSELF
Using AutoComplete

- Disable AutoComplete for user names and passwords on forms.

Identity Managers

Recent versions of the Microsoft operating system support the storage and management of your identity information and preferences in a capability known as Microsoft Passport. The Passport is created when you register for new software or for service support. When you access the website again, more information about you and your preferences is automatically added to the Passport.

The company's intent is to use this standard information about you each time you return to its website, complete a form or make a purchase on Microsoft's websites. However, the Passport is a useful source of your personal information if accessed by someone else. Therefore, it is generally accepted that the use and control of Passport-based information needs to be regulated and subject to regular review by government. Privacy laws and policy are discussed in Chapter 13.

ENCRYPTION

Encryption (also called encipherment) is the process of encoding data to prevent unauthorized access, especially during transmission over the Internet. The encrypted information or data is unreadable and meaningless until the person with the key unscrambles (decrypts) it.

You likely use encryption every day without realizing it. For example, you use it to protect your bankcard number and PIN each time you do an automated banking machine or point-of-sale direct debit transaction. You may not realize that encryption is used to protect your PIN and bankcard number and secure it as it travels the network. You also rely on encryption when you visit a secure website designated by the prefix of HTTPS, which indicates that the site uses SSL (Secure Socket Layers) encryption. HTTPS is discussed in Chapter 14.

You should consider using encryption to protect your files of personal, financial and private information that you store on your hard drive or removable media and to secure your e-mail transmissions, particularly when using a wireless LAN.

There are fundamentally two components to encryption:
- The algorithm that defines the strength of the scrambling (an analogy is the physical lock), and
- A numeric value or password (the key to the physical lock) that drives the scrambling and can be used to unlock the encrypted information.

Someone can only unscramble the information with the password/key and compatible encryption software.

Encrypting documents or files that include your personal, financial or private information is a secure way to prevent unauthorized persons from reading and misusing this information, as you control who may access and read this information. However, you must keep the key (usually a password) safe while the information is encrypted and safely communicate the key to the recipient who will use it to decrypt (unscramble) the information.

There are many software programs available for encrypting and decrypting documents and files. Some reputable security vendors have free copies available online for personal use.

Using Encryption Software

Make sure you fully understand the features of the encryption software and use it regularly to protect your sensitive information.

You will need to know how to:
- Load and install the software
- Configure the software, and
- Generate the encryption password/key.

Once you have installed the program, it should be a relatively simple process to activate it with your password/key, select the file of information you want to encrypt, and encrypt it. Some software also lets you digitally sign the information to prove later that nothing has changed or got lost. Digital signatures are discussed in Chapter 14.

The encrypted file could:

• Remain stored on your computer until you want to access it by decrypting it. Remember to encrypt the original file as well as the back-up copy, or
• Be sent as an e-mail attachment.

You can use this program to keep an encrypted file of all your personal and identity information, such as your bankcard number, credit card numbers, passport numbers, SIN, website identifiers/name and passwords. Be sure the file is kept in a safe place. You simply need to remember the password/key that will decrypt the file of all the other passwords. Also remember to encrypt sensitive information stored on back-up disks or on your personal web space or website.

Note: If you use encryption for personal use, the loss of your password could have significant consequences, as you would be unable to decrypt your documents and files. Create a passphrase, as it is easier to remember, such as the first letter of each word of your favourite poem or song. Passwords and passphrases are discussed in Chapter 10; tips for creating strong passwords and passphrases are included in the Resources section of this book.

Built-in Security Chips

Security chips are now being built into computers and are based on widely accepted standards. Increasingly, computer vendors, such as IBM, are offering this option. When the chip is built-in, the encryption and decryption functions are relatively simple to use and may include key recovery capabilities if you forget your password.

This discussion of encryption provides a basic overview. There are many sources of detailed information about encryption in books and on the Internet.

Low to Moderate Risk

If you are the only user of the encryption software, you simply need to remember the key or password and not disclose it to others. If you use encryption for protecting files that are transferred between you and others, such as encrypting document files to send in e-mail, the other users will need to have the compatible software with the same algorithm. Be careful when distributing the key or password to these other parties. This distribution must be done in a secure manner to prevent it from being disclosed to a third party. For example, call the person and provide the key over the telephone. Do NOT send the key by e-mail.

PRACTICAL STEPS TO PROTECT YOURSELF
Using Encryption Software

Technical steps to consider:

- Acquire and install encryption software and use it to encrypt all sensitive personal, financial and private information files.
- Use encryption software (or an embedded chip on your computer) to secure files of sensitive personal and financial information.
- Protect your encryption password or key and do not lose or forget it.

FIREWALLS

Firewalls monitor the Internet traffic to and from your computer and can filter or deflect unwanted actions, i.e., they protect your computer from unwanted intruders. For example, a firewall has the ability to detect a hacker attempting to invade your privacy and search your computer before any information is obtained or any damage is done. Similarly, if a program you have loaded, e.g., a financial management package, tries to connect out to the Internet to send or retrieve some information, the firewall will detect this action and give you the option to stop the transmission or allow it. A firewall will also prevent malicious software such as a Trojan horse sending information from your computer, including any captured keystrokes from the keyboard.

There are two types: software firewalls and hardware firewalls (more commonly known as routers). Each of these can be acquired for under $100 from many sources.

Software Firewalls

Software firewalls (often referred to as personal firewalls) are generally easy to install and configure but do require some maintenance. Once installed on your computer, the software monitors online traffic to and from it.

Look for a firewall that has the ability to:
- Produce a record of the approved traffic, e.g., linking your browser or e-mail software to the Internet and these connections flow without the continuous need for permission or giving warnings.
- Prevent any attempt to go out to the Internet that you do not authorize.
- Prompt you automatically about any new connections your computer makes, such as if your financial management package tries to access the Internet, which you can then allow or disallow the connection.
- Prompt you if some code attempts to access the Internet, such as a Trojan horse trying to send information about your keystrokes to the hacker that planted it.
- Remember the online access decisions you make for the next time so you are not asked for confirmation every time you go online, i.e., you can configure (instruct it) as to which online accesses are to flow through it without prompting for your approval.

A software firewall adds another level of control for others who may use your personal computer to access the Internet with it. Unless they know your password to the firewall, they can be prevented from going online.

Software Integrated Solution

Increasingly, virus scanners and software firewalls are being offered as software suites or integrated solutions, rather than as individual products. This approach is often more beneficial as they provide simplified help desks and greater capabilities for automatic updates. While the bundled suite may cost more, it is typically less expensive than purchasing individual products and the software in the suite is more likely to be compatible.

Hardware Firewall or Router

Hardware versions of a firewall, more commonly called a router, take more effort to set up than firewall software, as they require wires and their own power source. However, they are relatively inexpensive and relatively easy to install.

The additional protection of a hardware firewall is essential if your computer is:
- Continuously connected to the Internet, e.g., through a cable provider or DSL, or
- Part of a network of two or more computers (LAN or WLAN) that share Internet access.

The hardware firewall separates or segregates the network you use into different and distinct zones so that your computer and any associated network are secured in a restricted zone. This zone cannot be accessed through the firewall unless you allow the access. In essence, the firewall is a common gateway to the computers behind it and includes features that let you:
- Guard against outside attempts to penetrate your computer and network
- Manage access within your network between computers, and
- Provide a detailed activity log that shows all network log ins, including intrusion attempts.

Note: Many firewall solutions also perform other functions such as eliminating pop-up advertisements when you are browsing websites and preventing access to unwanted sites, such as adult or gambling sites that you may not want your children or other users accessing. There are many books and Internet websites that can provide more information on these capabilities.

Router Integrated Solution
High-risk computer owners should deploy both a hardware and software firewall and integrate them to ensure each computer behind the hardware firewall has a software firewall running that is compatible with the hardware firewall.

PRACTICAL STEPS TO PROTECT YOURSELF
Using a Firewall to Protect Your Internet Activity
- Install a software firewall on your computer that allows only the online activity you want to happen to and from the Internet. Configure it to allow your routine Internet activity and review its settings regularly.
- Install a hardware firewall (in addition to your software firewall). This is essential if you have a network of computers (LAN), cable or wireless. Routers are relatively inexpensive, fairly straightforward to install, and well worth the investment.

Technical step to consider:
- Integrate your hardware firewall with your software firewall and virus scanning software to ensure all are automatically present when you are online.

WIRELESS CONNECTIONS

Wireless is the technology that is predicted to significantly change the way we go about our daily lives and may further decrease the use of paper money. While pointing your cell phone at a vending machine to buy a soft drink or programming your fridge to order your groceries by talking to your computer are still futuristic uses, many wireless uses are already a reality.

Many users are attracted to the convenience of wireless, but they may not fully understand the deficiencies and potential risks. The wireless network and the use of wireless portable devices present risks that you need to assess carefully before you use wireless connections.

Wireless Networks

Although wireless networks have been available for some time, the high cost and the limitation of having to buy all of the equipment from the same manufacturer were initially a drawback. Now wireless standards have been developed that allow equipment from various manufacturers "to talk to each other". This interoperability combined with improved speed and range, greater affordability, and simpler set ups makes the flexibility of the wireless network attractive to many consumers.

Being able to connect to the Internet and all your computers without cables is very attractive and now relatively inexpensive. Not having to run lengths of cable to connect computers together saves time, money and in the home maintains the aesthetics of the home. Who wants to look at computer cables running from room to room? If your hardware firewall or router is in the basement, consider the difficulty of pulling cable from there to a computer on the second floor.

The most popular wireless systems are generally based on the physical firewall hardware previously discussed in this chapter. These devices are typically a router, with its own power supply. Instead of having to run cables between your computers, each computer has a small sender/receiver device that communicates with the router/firewall to create a wireless area network.

Wireless Security

Wireless networks have some significant inherent risks to your identity, privacy and money and also potentially to the safety of your home and family, e.g., an intruder intercepts your trip itinerary and plans a burglary or captures home webcams that are showing that no one is home.

Any device that lets you create a "wireless local area network" (or WLAN) should have the capability to encrypt all its traffic to and from the Internet and between all the computers linked to the network. This protection is essential as someone in close proximity to your home can easily capture your wireless communications.

You may recall when remote garage openers first became available that it was possible to drive by homes clicking the button looking for a garage opener on the same frequency. When one was found, the garage could be opened and the contents stolen. Similarly, people now drive around neighbourhoods and business areas with a computer and a wireless receiver that can detect signals from wireless communications. They can capture the information going across the wireless network and analyze it. If someone broke into your garage, you would notice the physical contents that were missing. However, if someone breaks into your wireless network, you will not know what personal information has been stolen and if the intrusion is continuing.

Wireless access points are increasingly available in public places; e.g., many coffee shops and hotels allow you to connect your laptop while enjoying their services. These connections are not automatically encrypted and you should assume that others can intercept your messages if you connect wirelessly. (These public access points are often referred to as wireless "hot spots".)

Therefore, security precautions for a wireless network are a very important consideration. Since the wireless network's radio waves are similar to those used for radio stations and cordless phones, the transmissions could be potentially intercepted by anyone with the right kind of receiver, on the same bandwidth and close enough, e.g., across the street, to access your network.

While it may appear that the transmission distance is say just 60 feet, this limit is a result of the smaller antennas embedded within the computer cards. If you don't take the proper security measures, a snoop with a larger antenna may be able to pick up your network's signal from as far away as several city blocks.

Emerging WEP Standard

As a first step for security, you need to ensure your wireless adaptors adhere to the IEEE 802.11 wireless standard. This standard provides several mechanisms for ensuring a secure operating environment but does not in itself prevent all possible misuse of the network. In particular, its encryption ability called WEP (Wired Equivalent Privacy) is intended to protect the confidentiality of your network traffic using the wireless protocol.

Depending on the manufacturer and the model of the card, there are different levels of WEP available. Further, new versions of the standard continue to improve the security. Version 802.11i is generally believed to be safer, where properly configured, than version 802.11b.

Keep in mind that for WEP to work, it has to be enabled at all of the access points of your wireless network. If the WEP is not enabled, intruders could access your wireless network.

Using Wireless for Web-based Services

Increasingly wireless pagers and cell phones are being used to send and receive e-mails, browse the Internet and do online financial transactions. Find out what security is built into the device or the applications you use on it.

Consider also that the wireless carrier is one more party that can access your information and may store it along the way. The wireless carrier that provides the communications between the device and the communications gateway that acts like an ISP and provides the link to the Internet. The good news is that properly engineered wireless devices have encryption capabilities built-in and as a result the communications between the device and the wireless gateway should be secure such that no one can pick your wireless "postcards" out of thin air.

However, as with all Internet communications, the security is not necessarily end-to-end, but rather to a specific point where your information is processed. From that point, the security may not exist or may be inadequate. Certainly where a specific purpose application is provided for the wireless device and you are authenticated to use the application, e.g., through an identifier/name and password, end-to-end encryption is likely in place.

High Risk
Generally, as the underlying security technology is not widely deployed and some technology may be safe and some may not be, all wireless activities must be considered high risk.

Also be cautious about doing personal transactions and computing on a WLAN at your place of work. Many people may have access to the encryption function and be able to re-configure it to access any personal information you communicate from your computer in the office. This could include your e-mail, your financial records and transactions, and any information you submit over the Internet.

PRACTICAL STEPS TO PROTECT YOURSELF
Using Wireless Connections

- Ensure that the wireless system has encryption/scrambling capabilities and that you properly configure them. You also need to check periodically that they are working.
- Only use wireless networks when you can control and configure the encryption on the link.
- Ask the wireless services provider to explain the security features of the wireless device in terms that you can understand. Seek assurance that it is the most current standard.
- Remember: All wireless activities must be considered high risk. Do NOT disclose sensitive information or do financial transactions on a WLAN unless you are certain the transmissions are secure.

16

CRISIS MANAGEMENT –
DEALING WITH
PERSONAL INFORMATION
LOSSES, ACCIDENTS AND
IDENTITY THEFT

Thousands of people are victims of identity theft each year. Identity theft goes far beyond the fraudulent use of your credit or debit cards or the theft of your physical mail. Each of these is an isolated and serious incident; however, each could also be a warning sign that someone is attempting to steal your identity.

This chapter details the steps you need to take in the event you suspect, or know, that someone is trying to hijack your identity or you have suffered an accident, such as the loss or theft of your wallet or credit card.

IDENTITY THEFT

Identity theft happens when information and documents about you have been disclosed or stolen and then used to generate documents and accounts and carry out transactions in your name. The identity thief goes about his or her daily life using your name, your finances and your credit rating. He or she becomes YOU. The thief may use your identity to lease an apartment or car, use your telephone banking to pay fraudulently obtained credit cards, or obtain a personal loan. Arrange for telephone and utility services, and carry out many other transactions in YOUR name. The hijacker could even get a job in your name.

If you are a victim of identify theft, you could face numerous problems that others, mainly creditors, will believe you have caused. For example:
• Delinquent accounts opened in your name for credit cards at financial services institutions or stores, for telephone, cell phone or ISP services, or for leasing or buying an automobile.
• Unpaid monthly rent on an apartment leased in your name.
• Driving offences using a driver's licence acquired in your name.

There have even been instances of identity thieves placing a mortgage on the victim's home or filing for bankruptcy under the victim's name to avoid eviction.

Is it Identity Theft?

If any of the following problems happen to you, does that mean that someone is trying to steal, or has stolen, your identity? Not necessarily. For example:
• You discover fraudulent charges on your credit card.

- You are unable to access to your telephone banking and you know your access code is correct.
- Money was transferred from your financial accounts that you did not authorize.
- You have lost or misplaced your wallet or purse, and then wonder if it was stolen.

Certainly these and similar situations are very worrisome and you need to take immediate action, but are they an indication of identity theft? The first step is to assess the situation to determine if it is a mistake or an accident, an isolated incident of theft or fraud, or an attack on your identity.

ASSESS THE SITUATION: ACCIDENT, LOSS OR CRISIS?

1. Determine whether the problem is an accident, loss, theft or an indication of identity theft.

You may have used your credit or debit card or made a payment that you simply forgot to record. You may have misplaced your debit or credit card or wallet. Before taking the next step, be sure of the facts; e.g., check suspicious transactions carefully or look again for your missing card or wallet. You do not want to take any steps that may be hard to undo. For example, you may simply have forgotten about the transaction. Contact your financial institution or other party and request the details. Your *Quick Contact List*, discussed in Chapter 2, will be helpful at this point.

2. If it is not a mistake and indeed is a problem, write down the details of the incident.

Many people forget the details of incidents when under stress. For example, where were you when your wallet was lost or stolen and what money and documents were in it? If the problem is a fraudulent transaction using your credit or debit card, where were you at that time on that day? Being able to show you were in another location at the time of the transaction can be very helpful.

3. Document conversations you have when reporting the problem.

When you report a loss or suspected fraud, be sure to write down the name of the person you spoke to and keep notes of the conversation.

4. Ask for the organization to send you written confirmation of your conversation.

When you contact an organization to report a problem, be sure to ask the representative to mail or fax you a written and signed confirmation of your conversation, or if that is not an option, to send an e-mail to you. Remember, the next time you contact the organization, you may speak to another employee who could deny or disagree with the actions agreed to by the first person you contacted. If this happens, follow up by sending a letter or fax detailing your initial report and the action the organization agreed to take. Request that the organization contact you immediately if they are in disagreement with any facts, as you have stated them, or if they believe facts have been omitted.

Moderate to High Risk
Carefully consider the number of problems or unusual events that are occurring. To have questionable or fraudulent charges on your credit card is one thing but to have that problem and another problem happening at the same time, such as discovering missing mail where the sender confirms that indeed the mail was sent, are a combination of circumstances that suggest a much higher risk.

PRACTICAL STEPS FOR CRISIS MANAGEMENT
Assessing the Situation
- Ensure that a problem exists. Perhaps you did make that credit card purchase or cash account withdrawal, but forgot about it. Check your records and your accounts again.
- If there is a problem, document the facts and keep notes of the conversations you have with those you must notify.
- Follow up with a written notification or report.
- Go on High Alert discussed as follows. Take action, but do not panic. This step is your safeguard.

TAKING ACTION: HIGH ALERT, POSSIBLE ATTACK, UNDER ATTACK
If you determine the incident or loss was not a mistake and may be more than an accident, the three stages you need to work through to assess and action what is happening and limit further damage include:
- **High Alert** – Take action at the first sign of a potential problem to reduce the likelihood of damages and losses.
- **Possible Attack** – Know what to do if you think you may be under attack.
- **Under Attack** – Know what to do if you know your identity is indeed being attacked.

HIGH ALERT

High Alert is an important safeguard; it is not a time to panic. It is a time to assess what has gone wrong and determine the facts. This can range all the way from discovering you have made an innocent error or something got lost in the mail through to a more serious problem.

Stay on High Alert until you can determine with certainty whether this is an isolated incident, e.g., a thief is using your credit card, or this is an indication of a more serious problem, that someone is taking steps to steal your identity.

PRACTICAL STEPS FOR CRISIS MANAGEMENT
Proceeding on High Alert
Carry out these steps as soon as you realize there is a problem. If your identity is not under attack, these actions are not things you will have to undo or ones that could have adverse consequences.

- Take action to resolve the particular problem that you have identified; e.g., phone your financial services provider if your credit card statement shows questionable charges. Take whatever steps are appropriate as advised throughout this book.
- Ask your financial services provider or other organization for advice. Explain what has happened and act on the advice given.
- Check the balances of your financial accounts and credit cards daily to determine if any unauthorized transactions are occurring.
- Change the PIN for all your bankcards, debit and credit cards, the access codes on your telephone banking, and the password to your online banking services, where appropriate.
- If you have a personal computer or use the Internet, review your *Personal Protection Plan* that you created when you did the risk assessment in Chapter 9. Make sure that you and all other users are stringently following these preventative strategies. Follow up on any problem areas.

POSSIBLE ATTACK

When you are on High Alert, you may find evidence that suggests that your identity MAY be under attack. This is a matter of judgment. There are no hard and fast rules. You have to consider the nature of the problem or problems that are occurring, the frequency and severity of each problem. Is there one unauthorized charge on your debit card or are there several of high value within one day? Are there different types of problems occurring (e.g., both your debit card and credit card reflect transactions you have not made)?

PRACTICAL STEPS FOR CRISIS MANAGEMENT
Proceeding on Possible Attack

The practical steps you should take when you suspect your identity MAY be under attack include all of the steps above in the High Alert stage, plus these important steps:

- Contact your financial services provider and other providers.

  Inform them about your concerns around your personal and financial information. Heed their advice. Consider replacing your debit and credit cards, changing your bank accounts and getting new chequebooks, and selecting new PINs, passwords and access codes. You may also want to temporarily discontinue using telephone or online banking to limit your risk exposure.

- Contact the credit bureaus.

  Inform them you think your identity is under attack. Ask them to inform you about any credit checks being done on your name or new credit accounts being reported. This is an important step because the hijacker may be using your name and documents to apply for loans, leases or carry out other transactions that would result in queries to the credit bureau. Check your credit report.

  As discussed in Chapter 6, look in the white pages of your telephone book or go to the websites of the credit bureaus:

Equifax Canada	www.equifax.com
TransUnion Canada	www.tuc.ca

UNDER ATTACK

If evidence shows that your identity is Under Attack, you should perform all of the steps above as well as those that follow. The identity thief may have already obtained loans or opened accounts in your name.

PRACTICAL STEPS FOR CRISIS MANAGEMENT
Proceeding Under Attack

- Report the crime to the local police immediately.

  Ask for a copy of the police report so that you can provide proof of the theft to the organizations involved. Provide the police with the names and phone numbers of all people you have contacted about your identity being under attack. This will improve the flow of information and increase the chances that the person will be apprehended quickly.

- Contact PhoneBusters, the central agency in Canada that collects and disseminates information on identity theft complaints and facilitates prosecution. Telephone: 1-888-495-8501; website: www.phonebusters.com
- Take steps to undo the damage. If fraudulent transactions involving your name have occurred, you will have a lot of work to do to rectify the situation.

  Chapters 6 and 7 provided guidance on dealing with organizations and financial services providers. However, fraudulent transactions may have been carried out in your name with financial service providers or companies with which you have never done business. This situation is the most difficult of all.

  The good news is that as you start to clean up these problems, those organizations that verify you have been defrauded can be asked to provide a letter or act as a reference as you proceed to contact others to convince them that the lease, the credit card bill or the debt has not been authorized by you but rather by someone using your identity.

- Heed the expert advice provided by the police, financial services institutions and organizations that you contact.

- Stay on High Alert.

  Until the police have apprehended the identity thief, you must stay on High Alert. The criminal may attempt to use your identity repeatedly locally as well as in other cities and countries. The credit bureaus are a good source of help as generally they receive all requests for credit. Once they have annotated your credit report to reflect the identity theft, they will be very helpful in curtailing the damage.

- Write detailed notes and safeguard these with copies of all related documents. You need to document everything that occurs.

  You will need to share this information with the police, your financial service institution and other organizations. They have impressive resources for following up and stopping credit and bank fraud of all kinds.

- Avoid companies that claim to repair bad credit.

  Some of these "credit-repair" companies charge steep fees and may not improve the client's credit rating in any way. There have also been cases of this type of company offering to establish credit under a new identity – a fraudulent act in itself.

RESPONDING TO SPECIFIC, ISOLATED LOSSES, ACCIDENTS AND PROBLEMS

As discussed previously, the first step is to deal with the impact of the specific problem or accident that has occurred. Throughout the chapters of this book, the many practical steps provided should help you address specific risk exposures. But accidents and theft still happen.

This section details the practical steps need to take when responding to a specific loss, accident or problem. Again, the three stages of High Alert, Possible Attack and Under Attack, as previously discussed, are also applicable at the various stages of dealing with an incident.

Again, there are no hard and fast rules. In every instance, you will need to use your personal judgment in assessing a specific situation and determining how to proceed. It is important to take appropriate, prompt action. Above all, avoid panic and proceed calmly and carefully. As you read the sections below, also keep in mind that the occurrences may be isolated concerns or may indicate the start of an attack on your identity. You have to consider the frequency and severity with which each particular type of problem occurs, and the number of different types of problems that may be going on at the same time.

LOST, MISSING OR UNEXPECTED MAIL

Pay attention to your billing cycle and the expected arrival dates of important documents. If you do not receive important mail as expected or you receive statements or acknowledgements from providers or organizations with which you do not do business, take action immediately.

The latter situation can be quite serious. If you receive a notice that you have applied for a debit or credit card, applied for a loan or receive acknowledgement of a purchase or lease of which you have no knowledge, it is quite possible that your identity is being used by someone else and that the confirmation has been sent to your address.

PRACTICAL STEPS FOR CRISIS MANAGEMENT
Responding to Problems with your Mail
If important mail does not arrive when expected:

- Verify that the provider or organization actually sent the mail to you.

   If it was sent, is the mail simply lost or have you been missing other pieces of mail? If other mail has not arrived as expected in the recent past, someone may be trying to gather information about you and your documents on a regular basis. While you should regularly do a visual check of your mailbox and mail to see if there are any signs of tampering, be aware that the skilful thief can rifle your mail and not leave any traces.

- Consider the nature of the missing mail. Notify the applicable creditors and government agencies.

Did you expect to receive a replacement credit or debit cards, a passport or driver's licence, your SIN card or other mail that would contain documents or information that someone could use to masquerade as you? Notify the applicable financial services institution, creditor or government agency immediately. Your *Quick Contact List* will be helpful for taking quick action.

- Call Canada Post if you suspect someone is diverting your mail.
- Go on High Alert.

If you are missing several pieces of mail or missing mail on more than one occasion, as a minimum, go on High Alert. Also consider taking the steps for responding to a Possible Attack.

If you receive statements or acknowledgements from providers or creditors with whom you do not do business:

- Contact the sender immediately.

Determine if, in fact, the person or organization thinks they are dealing with you, despite the fact you have not been involved with them.

- If you determine someone is using your identity to deal with this organization or provider, immediately follow the steps for High Alert, Possible Attack and Under Attack.

LOSS OR THEFT OF YOUR DEBIT AND CREDIT CARDS

If you lose your debit and/or credit cards, your money or credit is at risk. As a minimum, go on High Alert until such time that you locate your cards. Theft is, of course, more serious since the thief obviously intends to use your cards.

PRACTICAL STEPS FOR CRISIS MANAGEMENT
Responding to the Loss or Theft of Your Debit and Credit Cards

If you lose or misplace your credit or debit card:
- Follow the steps for High Alert.
- Check every possible location — your wallet, your briefcase, your desk, the last merchant or restaurant you visited, your desk and every place you may have used or left the card.
- If you cannot locate your card, follow the steps for a Possible Attack.

If your debit or credit card is missing from your custody and not readily found:
- Immediately notify your financial services provider that your cards are missing and may be stolen, not lost. Have the card deactivated immediately.
- Follow all of the steps for Possible Attack.

LOSS OR THEFT OF YOUR WALLET OR PURSE

The loss of your wallet and/or purse is a very serious risk exposure as you may have lost not only money and your debit and credit cards, but also your driver's licence, your SIN card and possibly other documents that provide a great deal of information about you, such as your car registration and your cheque book. These documents may contain sufficient information for the thief to hijack your identity. As discussed in Chapter 2, the best preventative step for protecting yourself is to minimize the number of cards and documents that you carry with you in the first place.

PRACTICAL STEPS FOR CRISIS MANAGEMENT
Responding to Loss or Theft of Your Wallet or Purse

If you lose or misplace your wallet or purse:
- Follow the steps for High Alert.
- Check every possible location — every room in your home, your car, the last merchant or restaurant you visited, and every place you recently visited.
- If your wallet or purse contains many items that would be useful for an identity thief, consider following the steps under Possible Attack.

If your wallet or purse is stolen:
- Immediately notify the police.
- Follow the steps for Possible Attack.

UNAUTHORIZED FINANCIAL TRANSACTIONS OR DENIAL OF CREDIT

Unfortunately, unauthorized charges on credit cards are becoming increasingly commonplace. If you followed the practical steps presented in Chapter 4, hopefully only your secondary card is being misused.

If you are denied credit on your credit card or a withdrawal with your debit card and you believe that your credit should be in good standing, this could be an indication that someone is masquerading as you and using your credit and money.

PRACTICAL STEPS FOR CRISIS MANAGEMENT
Responding to Unauthorized Charges and Financial Transactions or Denial of Credit
- Follow the steps for High Alert.
- Change your debit card PINs, access codes and passwords.
- Consider discussing the situation more thoroughly with your financial services provider.
- If credit requests have been made that you did not initiate or authorize, immediately follow the steps for Possible Attack.

PRIVATE INFORMATION BECOMES PUBLIC

You may not be aware of just how much information about you is available in the public domain. There is little you can do except to be aware of the information that is available (such as searching your name on the Internet) and to take steps to ensure organizations and providers are in compliance with the protection afforded in federal and provincial privacy legislation. Chapter 6 discusses legislated information disclosure and the protections afforded in the federal *Personal Information Protection and Electronic Documents Act 2000* (PIPEDA).

However, if the information leak has originated from an agency, organization or provider with whom you have been dealing in confidence, you can take steps to limit the damage and stop further leaks of information. An information leak could range from someone obtaining an unlisted phone number, to someone knowing about your medical treatments, your tax liability, or your financial account and loan balances.

PRACTICAL STEPS FOR CRISIS MANAGEMENT
Dealing with An Information Leak
- Determine the source of the information leak. This may be evident from the nature of the information.
- Contact the agency, provider or organization and ask how the information could have been leaked.
- Ask for the name of the person in the organization who deals with these complaints, often the enterprise's Privacy Officer. Contact this person, and inquire about the process for protecting your privacy. The organization should immediately investigate the information leak and take steps to ensure information about you does not again become public.

Dealing with Inaccurate or Incomplete Information

This problem is more complex if the information being provided about you is inaccurate, incomplete or out-of-date.

- Work backwards from the person or company that has wrong or incomplete information about you to determine the original source.
- Contact the source of the information and work with them to ensure corrections are made and the information is updated.
- Ask the department or organization to send you a confirmation that your personal information has been updated appropriately.

PROTECTING YOURSELF IN TODAY'S WORLD

No matter how careful you are, the risk of someone invading your privacy, stealing your money, damaging your credit record, attempting to misuse or successfully hijacking your identity is an everyday reality.

While there are no measures that will guarantee your safety, the advice presented throughout this book can help you recognize and reduce your risks, limit the potential for theft, loss and misuse, and respond quickly and effectively if, despite these precautions, you are a victim.

Now that you have read this book, you have the skills and knowledge that will enable you to proactively take control of your most sensitive personal and financial information and consistently protect your money, privacy and identity. The broad range of practical protect-yourself steps offered throughout these chapters will help you achieve these goals with relatively little inconvenience and cost. Indeed, in many cases, simply questioning requests and processes and knowing your rights will take you a long way! So take control, stay informed, continuously assess your risks and practices and become a victor, not a victim, of the Information Age.

RESOURCES

RESOURCE 1
YOUR INFORMATION LISTS — WORKED EXAMPLES

The worked examples of the *Quick Contact List* and the *Personal Information List* are aids to help you record and keep safe all the useful contact information that you may need infrequently, yet is critical in an emergency. As you can see, the examples go beyond financial contacts to include other telephone numbers that may be needed in a family emergency.

EMERGENCY INFORMATION — YOUR QUICK CONTACT LIST
Break open in emergencies ... but check it regularly.
The information that you record on this list is largely public and not the sensitive personal information that others could use to harm you if it is found or stolen. Make multiple copies of the smaller *Quick Contact List* and keep copies in your vehicles, with your passports, and even with a family member or friend who you could contact if all other copies are inaccessible or lost, for example, when you are travelling. The list can also be "shrunk" to wallet size and laminated.

Use this example as a template to build your own list and ensure you keep it current and with you at all times.

Quick Contact List — A worked example

Contact Information for:	Telephone #s from Home	In Canada	Outside North America	Date Last Checked
My Bank – XYZ Bank Contact John Brown	416 Z99 2888	800 4MY BANK	416 Z88 9999	April
My Primary Credit Card	800 4MY BANK	800 4MY BANK	416 Z88 4999	April
My Secondary Credit Card	800 4MY BANK	800 4MY BANK	416 Z88 4999	April
My Tears Card	800 401 STOR	800 401 STOR	905 Z22 1111	April
My Canadian Tube Card	800 402 STOR	800 402 STOR	905 333 Z222	April
My Shesso Gas Token Device # 1234 4321	888 GAS TOKN	888 GAS TOKN	None	April
My Home Alarm Company	416 Z22 1111	416 Z22 1111	416 Z22 1111	January
My Birth Certificate	416 325 8305	800 461 2156	416 325 8305	May
My SIN Card	800 206 7218	800 206 7218	506 548 7961	May
My Health Card	416 314 5518	416 314 5518	416 314 5518	May
My Passport 1999 Toronto	416 973 3215	800 567 6868	416 973 3215	May
My Driver's Licence	Visit the Local Licensing Office			May
My Car Insurance ZYX Co – Mary Policy # 1234567	416 999 Z222	800 COVERAG	416 999 1111 collect	January
My House Insurance XYZ Bank – Tom Policy # 7654321	416 999 Z222	800 COVERAG	416 999 1111 collect	January
My Medical Insurance GNI Insurance Policy # 123 787 321	416 999 Z222	800 COVERAG	416 999 1111 collect	January
My ISP Dial-up	416 Z65 9999	800 4MY DIAL	800 4MY DIAL	May
My Children's School	416 Z89 1111	416 Z89 1111	416 Z89 1111	September
Bell Canada Directory Assistance	411	411	Contact local Canada Direct	January
Identity Theft Notification Credit Bureaus	800 465 7166 877 525 2823	800 465 7166 877 525 2823	514 493 2314 905 527 0401	January
Police – Local Division	416-999-9999			May
PhoneBusters[1]	888-495-8501	888-495-8501		May

[1] PhoneBusters is the central agency in Canada that collects and disseminates information on identity theft complaints and facilitates prosecution. For more information, go to www.phonebusters.com

YOUR PERSONAL INFORMATION LIST

The *Personal Information List* is a master list on which you should record the very sensitive personal information that expands on the limited contact information you have recorded on your *Quick Contact List*. Use this example as a template to create your own list. Remember you must store the *Personal Information List* in a very secure place, such as in your home safe or a safety deposit box, as this list contains information that would certainly put your money, privacy, and identity at risk if it were lost or stolen.

Personal Information List — A worked example

Contact Information for:	Telephone #s From Home	In Canada	Outside North America	Date Last Checked
My Bank — John Brown Account # 001 Account # 002 Debit Card #### ### ####	416 Z99 2888	800 4MY BANK	416 Z88 9999	April
My Primary Credit Card #### ### ### ##	800 4MY BANK	800 4MY BANK	416 Z88 4999	April
My Secondary Credit Card #### ### ### ###	800 4MY BANK	800 4MY BANK	416 Z88 4999	April
My Tears Card #### ### ### ###	800 401 STOR	800 401 STOR	905 Z22 1111	April
My Canadian Tube Card #### ### ### ###	800 402 STOR	800 402 STOR	905 333 Z222	April
My Shesso Gas Card #### ### ### ###	888 GAS STAT	888 GAS STAT	None	April
My Shesso Gas Token Device # 1234 4321	888 GAS TOKN	888 GAS TOKN	None	April
My Home Alarm Company	416 Z22 1111	416 Z22 1111	416 Z22 1111	January
My Birth Certificate #### #### Spouse = #### ####	416 325 8305	800 461 2156	416 325 8305	May
My Citizenship Card #### ### Spouse #### ###	800 255 4541	800 255 4541	None	May
My SIN Card ### ### ### Spouse = ### ### ###	800 206 7218	800 206 7218	506 548 7961	May
My Health Card #### ### ## Spouse = #### ### ###	416 314 5518	416 314 5518	416 314 5518	May
My Passport ### ###### 1999 Toronto	416 973 3215	800 567 6868	416 973 3215	May
Spouse's Passport ### ###### 1999 Toronto	416 973 3215	800 567 6868	416 973 3215	May
My Driver's Licence #### #### ####	Visit the Local Licensing Office			May
Spouse's Driver's Licence #### #### ####	Visit the Local Licensing Office			May

RESOURCE 2
CREATING STRONG PINs, PASSWORDS AND PASSPHRASES

Many times people complain that they have too many passwords, access codes and PINs yet are typically expected to remember them all without writing them down! (This is discussed further in Resource 3.)

Often the provider will give you the passwords and PINs, making them more difficult to remember as you did not select them and you may not be able to change them. Further, you are advised not to make up passwords using common information, e.g., your date of birth or a simple word, e.g., "apples". In fact, many systems prevent you from doing this. You are advised to create long, rambling, unpredictable passwords that are difficult for others to guess. This advice is unrealistic, particularly given the number of passwords most people must use in their daily lives. However, the alternative of writing them down, as a habit, and keeping them current is dangerous and an accident waiting to happen.

An important benefit of passphrases is that can they can be written in a hidden secret code and not likely found or guessed. You could include a simple page of phrases and obscure lists of words and numbers in your wallet, purse or address book that would be difficult for someone else to decipher. And, even if someone did find this page, it is unlikely that the person would get it right the first time. It would take several tries to find the passphrase and even then it may not be successful.

Examples of ways to create strong passphrases include:

• Use the first letter of a well-known phrase, saying, hymn, poem or novel, etc.:

"MHALL" representing "Mary had a little lamb". Of course, this is not effective if your name is M. Hall!

"ADTFIAT" representing "and did those feet in ancient times" is better; it could even be remembered as an alarm company "ADT" and a car company "FIAT"!

- Modify a simple phrase: "I love my dog Fluffy".

  There are many options including:
  — Changing letters for numbers e.g. "l" for 1 or "g" for 8 such that you have "1l0v3myd08fluffy".
  — Eliminating the vowels "lvmydgflffy"
  — Changing the spelling "Eye luv mi dog phlufie"
  — A combination of the first letter and numbers being "1lmdF"

The options and combinations are endless, particularly when you use a phrase that includes numbers and you change it periodically. For example, "1lmdF" could become "1l2kmdF" if you need more than six characters in the passphrase. Decide whether "2k" means "to kiss" or "to kick".

RESOURCE 3
DISGUISING YOUR PINs AND PASSWORDS

The agreements of some financial services and other service providers stipulate that you may not write down your passwords or PINs, while others allow you to write them down if they are disguised. Increasingly, security policies and agreements are allowing this latter approach.

Most people have too many passwords, PINs, access codes and other secret numbers, yet are advised to make them all different. Realistically, unless they are used almost daily, people cannot be expected to remember them all. Many authorities strongly advise that a password or PIN be selected that is easy to remember but hard for someone else to guess. For example, you should not use a password with all the same numbers i.e., 111111, as it is easily guessed or seen by someone who is shoulder surfing. Digits that are part of your identity, e.g., your date of birth, or part of your driver's licence should also be avoided.

Many people write passwords and PINs down and put them in places that do not seem obvious to them. However, thieves know all the tricks and hiding places and frequently can find a PIN written down in a stolen wallet or purse, and use it with the victim's stolen bankcard. Should your financial services provider find that you have written down your PIN, it will likely make you liable for any money taken from your accounts by the thief, even where there is a videotape of the person taking the money from your account, and it was not you! Thus, protecting your PIN is vital and not writing it down is essential, although not really practical for everyone.

Where an agreement or policy allows passwords or PINs to be recorded, then write it in a hidden or disguised manner that only you can decipher. Used for centuries to hide secret information, the technique is known as steganography (meaning hidden writing). Write it in a way that only you know and then hide it. There are many ways to do this and, if you invent your own, you just need to remember how you did it and not tell anyone else.

For example:

- Include your PIN as a non-existent telephone number in your wallet or address book. Since a thief presumably does not know your relatives and friends or the places where you do business, disguising your password as a fake telephone number will deter the thief from using your stolen debit card. A false entry for Aunt Hyacinth or your favourite florist, Hyacinth's, could have the telephone number 905-265-4183. It does not matter if the number actually exists.

This false telephone number could disguise a PIN that is:
- — 4183 — the last four digits
- — 3814 — the last four digits backwards
- — 0251 — alternate numbers starting at the second number
- — 3152 — alternative numbers starting at the last number backwards.

- Include your password or PIN in a box of numbers that appear to be random and only you know the starting point to get into the box to get at your PIN.

For example:

```
4 2 3 1
5 1 9 0
2 4 8 6
8 2 5 3
```

If your PIN is 4183, an easy way to remember this is to visualize entering a familiar room at the top left hand corner (for example, this could the location of the door in your bedroom) and moving diagonally to the farthest corner. Your PIN would be 4183. If you moved to all four corners, again it would be 4183. If you entered by the door three-quarters of the way down the right hand wall and moved directly to the opposite wall, your PIN would be 6842.

The secret here is the thief may find the box of numbers but may not know what it is (unless they have read this book!). In any case, the many combinations are a deterrent to the thief's accessing your account.

Note: **Your bank will more likely believe that you did not write down your PIN if the thief does not successfully enter your PIN the first time he or she uses your bankcard. Successful first time access indicates that the PIN was easy to obtain or guess.**

The examples discussed here are for illustration purposes and you are encouraged to develop your own approach to disguising your password or PINs. If you invent a personal method, you will more likely remember it and it is very unlikely that the thief will have seen it before or can guess it. Remember to always select passwords, passphrases and PINs that are easy for you to remember and disguise, yet difficult for someone to guess or discover.

RESOURCE 4
PROTECTING YOUR ELECTRONIC
FINANCIAL SERVICES

The *Ultimate 'Safety PIN' Checklist* provides guidelines and principles for managing and protecting your use of electronic financial services, including your
bankcards (debit and credit cards), ABMs, point-of-sale, telephone banking,
online banking and brokerage, your PINs, access code, passwords and passphrases.

There are many lists on how to protect your bankcards and PINs. Some are simple "Do's and Don'ts" of four or five items of advice. Others are more detailed,
and some are just not very helpful, e.g. "hide your PIN"!

After reviewing the best advice we could find and adding some tips of our own,
we created the *Ultimate Safety PIN Checklist*. We acknowledge that we have
included tips from other sources including the Canadian banks, the Canadian
Bankers Association and Interac Association to create a complete and comprehensive checklist.

**Note: Many of the steps in this checklist are applicable to your other electronic
activities and risks.**

For the purposes of this checklist, the term PIN relates to the code (usually at
least four digits) used with your debit card (and potentially your credit card) at
ABMs, stores and restaurants, etc. The term "access code" relates to the code
used to access your telephone banking service. The terms "password" and
"passphrase" (usually a stronger code of at least seven digits) relate to those used
to access online Internet-based financial services. Generically, access codes,
passwords and passphases are referred to as "codes" in this checklist unless stated otherwise.

PRACTICAL STEPS AND PRINCIPLES TO PROTECT YOURSELF AND YOUR ELECTRONIC FINANCIAL SERVICES

The Ultimate Safety Pin Checklist

DO

- ✓ Continuously safeguard your bankcards, PINs and codes; they are the keys to your financial services and credit accounts.
- ✓ Only use PINs and codes that you have personally created.
- ✓ Use separate and distinct PINs and codes for your debit card, telephone banking, and online banking services.
- ✓ Choose PINs and codes that are easy to remember and disguise, but difficult for others to guess or find.
- ✓ Limit the number of accounts linked to your debit card. It is wise to link only your chequing account and NOT your savings accounts where you likely have more money at risk. Check whether your financial services provider automatically linked all your accounts to your bankcard when it was issued.

DO NOT

When creating your PINs or codes, do NOT use:

- ✗ Obvious information such as your name, telephone number, date of birth, etc.
- ✗ Any number sequence that appears on your personal documents, such as your social insurance card or driver's licence number.
- ✗ The same sequences of numbers and/or letters for your debit card, telephone banking and online banking services.
- ✗ The sequences of numbers that appear on your financial transactions, such as the last four digits of your credit card or your bank account number.

Change Your PIN and Codes

✓ Each time you receive a new or replacement debit card, be sure to create a new PIN and sign the back of the card where required.

✓ Change your PINs and codes regularly, depending on your usage, e.g., every six months. If you use your debit card and PIN almost daily and make many debit payments, change it more frequently.

✓ Only change your PIN at your financial services institution or at one of their branded ABMs.

✓ When changing your PIN, always be aware of your surroundings particularly when using a branded ABM. Check to see if security cameras could be capable of recording your keystrokes. Specifically, turn your back towards the camera and block its view of the keypad. If you are unsure whether the location is safe to change your PIN, go elsewhere.

✓ If you will be using your PIN while travelling, change it before and after your trip.

✓ Only use the same service you are accessing to change that PIN or code. Use the telephone to change only your telephone banking access code and use the Internet to change your online banking password or passphrase.

✗ Never change your bankcard PIN over the telephone or by using online banking.

✓ If you must use a cordless telephone or cell phone to change your access code, be sure to change your access code as soon as possible afterwards using a more secure landline telephone.

Disclosure and Usage

✗ Generally, you should never write your PIN down in plain text. Where your financial services agreement permits the use of hidden writing techniques to disguise your PIN, use a method that only you know to conceal your PIN.

✓ PINs must be disguised within the written record so that no one can easily guess or find them.

✗ Never disclose your PIN or codes to anyone. Representatives from a financial services institution, the police or a merchant should not ask for your PIN; you are the only person who should know it. If a service officer or manager at your financial services institution contacts you or you have personally contacted them, disclose only your debit card number and the multi-digit card verification value. Never disclose your PIN or codes.

✗ Never lend your debit card and PIN to anyone to do a transaction for you, including a family member or close friend.

✗ Never allow someone else to enter your PIN, including a merchant, when completing a transaction. Unlike a credit card, your debit card should never disappear from your custody when buying something.

✗ Do not write your telephone banking access code near or on a telephone.

✓ Always conduct your ABM transactions when and where you feel most secure. If you are uncomfortable about using the ABM for any reason, do your transactions later or go to another location.

✓ To ensure privacy when conducting an ABM or debit transaction, use your hand or body as a shield to prevent others from observing you entering your PIN. Make sure no one is standing behind you or loitering near you. Consider touching but not depressing some additional keys that are not part of your PIN to confuse anyone trying to "shoulder surf" you to obtain your PIN.

✓ Where your personal space at the automated banking machine or merchant point-of-sale debit terminal is being "cramped", politely request people to move or turn away while you complete your transaction so that they can not "shoulder surf" to obtain your PIN.

✓ Be conscious of people loitering and generally hanging around you at the automated banking machine, even where they appear to be security guards or work persons such as window washers with an apparent need to be there. Be very cautious when using ABMs in shopping malls or in bank branch lobbies, particularly when the branch is closed.

✓ Be particularly cautious when using a drive-through ABM. Ensure your vehicle doors are locked and take extra care to shield your PIN entry.

✓ Be aware of the "switch and bait" trick at an ABM where someone distracts you by saying you dropped a $20 bill and switches your debit card as it comes out from the machine.

...

✓ Be aware of surveillance security cameras that may be directed at you when entering your PIN, such as in a gas station booth or store. The camera should not be pointed at you in such a way that it could record your PIN as you enter it. Turn your back towards the camera to block its view of the keypad. If you are unsure whether the location is safe, do not complete your transaction at that location.

✓ Check that your PIN number is not displayed by any device at any time.

✓ Check that your debit card number, credit card number and account numbers are not printed in full on your transaction receipts. These numbers should only be shown with several characters masked-out, for example by "****". Only a few digits should be printed to help you determine the number for yourself.

✓ If you are held up at an ABM, remember that your safety comes first. Co-operate with the robber's request and immediately report the incident to the police and to your financial services institution.

✓ Check that there is only one wire or cable connecting the PIN entry device when making a debit payment at a point-of-sale.

✓ Use the "Cancel" button to stop your transaction, retrieve your card and leave immediately if you feel unsafe or observe suspicious activity.

After Using Your Card

✓ After completing an ABM or debit transaction, remember to take your card and, if provided, your transaction record with you.

✗ Do not stand and count your cash at the ABM. Put your cash, card and transaction record into your pocket or wallet immediately and leave.

✓ Treat your transaction receipts as "toxic waste". Do not discard them carelessly. Store them safely and be sure to destroy them after reconciling your account.

✓ Be the detective yourself and, at least once a month, reconcile all of your financial accounts and statements for your credit cards that are linked to your debit card. Immediately report any unexplained transactions to your financial services institution, including deposits, which may be the start of a fraud by someone using your bankcard.

If Your Card is Lost, Stolen or Retained by an ABM

✓ If your debit card is lost, stolen or retained by an ABM, notify your financial services institution immediately. Most financial service institutions offer 1-800 telephone numbers and/or a 24-hour service for reporting lost or stolen cards.

Note: **Few financial services agreements require you to notify them when a machine retains your debit card! Check your agreement, but report it anyway.**

✓ If an ABM retains your debit card, be very wary if a stranger is overly helpful. Continuously re-entering your PIN will NOT recover your card. Using the "Cancel" button may return it.

✓ Always contact your financial services institution directly to report a lost, stolen or retained debit card and use a telephone number that you know is correct. Do not use a telephone number or cell phone that a stranger offers.

✓ Keep the emergency contact numbers for your financial services institution handy. Program them into your cell phone. Note that if you plan to use your debit card while travelling outside of Canada, the provider's toll-free 1-800 number may not work. Be sure to take the provider's local number so you can make a long distance call in an emergency. Many financial services institutions will accept the long distance charges.

Ask Your Financial Services Provider

When selecting a financial services institution, ask questions about the services they can provide with the use of your accounts, PINs and access codes.

Ask if they have the capability to allow you to:
✓ Decide the length of your PINs and codes, i.e., use more than the customary four digits?
✓ Select different and distinct PINs for different services, including debit card usage, telephone banking and online Internet banking?
✓ Select different PINs for each of your debit cards and credit cards?

...

✓ Choose your own personal PIN and codes, and be able to change these regularly and conveniently?

✓ Decide the number of invalid attempts with your PIN or codes before your access is temporarily unusable for, say, 24 hours? (You should try to get this limit set to three tries.)

✓ Determine the withdrawal limits on your accounts where you want them to be less than the financial services institution's standard limits, i.e., less than $1,000 per day?

✓ Specify that your debit card cannot be used in certain locations, such as outside Canada or in casinos?

✓ Set up an "emergency use/alarm" PIN or code that you can use when under duress to make a limited withdrawal for, say, $100 "due to technical problems"?

✓ Set up additional PINs and codes to make withdrawals from certain accounts, e.g., your savings account?

✓ Limit the accounts that are linked to your bankcard?

✓ Permanently opt out of alternative delivery systems such as telephone banking or online banking?

Note: As no major Canadian financial services institution currently provides all these services, perhaps the ultimate "safety PIN" tip is to ask why these services are not available. As customers, we need to communicate that these services are needed and point out how they could help us protect our money, privacy and identity.

For further information about this topic, refer to the Canadian Code of Practice for Consumer Debit Card Services that can be obtained from the Interac Association.

Interac Association	www.interac.ca
Canadian Bankers Association	www.cba.ca
Canadian Payments Association	www.cdnpay.ca

Resource 5
PERSONAL PROTECTION PLAN — COMPUTING AND ONLINE: A WORKED EXAMPLE

Chapter 9 discussed the *Basic Protection Plan* and outlined the *Personal Protection Plan* that everyone should create to protect their computing and online activities. This Resource provides a worked example of a *Personal Protection Plan* for a low-risk user.

LR is a young professional who works for a financial institution and who has some very disciplined habits. She owns a desktop computer that is two years old, with the standard 2000 operating system. Additionally, her computer has software that lets her do word processing, spreadsheets, browse the Internet and send and receive e-mail. Her computer was preloaded with all this software, as well as a virus scanner software from a reputable vendor and some games.

LR is generally the only person to use her personal computer. However, occasionally she has family visitors that she allows to use it.

LR is a long-standing member of her church's outreach group and keeps their financial and donation records on the spreadsheet software. She uses a graphics package she bought and loaded herself to create posters and flyers.

LR is also a games player in that she plays against her computer software in solo, bridge and chess.

LR has a basic ISP plan that gives her 30 hours of online dial-up access each month. Her browsing habits involve simply searching information, mainly around investments and charities, and obtaining news, etc. She occasionally downloads electronic forms and other information. She uses online banking, and sends and receives about 25 e-mails each month, including the exchange of family photographs.

LR regularly reviews her risk assessment in relation to her computing and online activities and has assessed her risk as "low".

LR's actions to protect her computing and online activities have been implemented in her *Personal Protection Plan*, explained below. Of note is she has incorporated some "moderate risk" protection steps into her Plan to reflect one or two moderate risk activities, e.g., online money transfer.

LR's Personal Protection Plan — for computing and online

LR's Personal Computer Protection

LR uses her computer's standard 2000 operating system and available software security features:

- LR has set up a personal administrator ID such that only she can install or remove software, make software changes, and add other components. She rarely does these things.
- She has set up a Guest ID for her family visitors who may use her personal computer.
- She changes personal and guest passwords every six months.
- She has changed the default system password for the e-mail software and selected her own password. She changes it every six months.
- She checks for operating system and browser security releases and patches every month online and uses the auto-detection capabilities where available. She applies updates and fixes each month.
- She does not use freeware.

LR's Guest Users' Protection

- LR's guests may use web-based e-mail using the browser software, browse the Internet and play the computer games.
- LR's guests are generally low or moderate risk users. She has "posted" this *Personal Protection Plan* and other rules near her computer based on the activities she would expect them to do in respecting her computer and Internet access, e.g., do not disable password checkers and virus scanners, do not download freeware from any source, and do not open e-mail from an unknown source, particularly those with an attachment.

LR's Electronic Identification Protection

- LR always selects passphrases that are easy for her to remember and disguise, yet difficult for someone else to guess or discover.
- Her passphrases are at least seven characters in length.
- She never discloses her passwords/passphrases to anyone and only records them in a disguised or hidden manner as a back up. She keeps the back up in a sealed envelope locked in her personal home safe/lock box.
- She changes her passphrases every six months in May (her birthday) and November (her sister's birthday).

LR's Virus Protection

- LR uses the virus scanner software that came preloaded on her computer and is from a reputable vendor.
- She has registered it and pays for annual renewals online using her credit card.
- She keeps the virus scanner current with new releases and updates monthly using the automated notification feature.
- She always downloads and updates virus definition files when new ones are available.
- She has configured her virus scanner to be active on her computer's start-up and to scan continuously in "background" mode, including when she opens e-mails. Her ISP also virus scans her e-mail.
- She scans her computer (all files, programs and hard drives) on the first day of every month at 9:00 p.m. in the evening (unless it is a weekend when she does it on the first Monday of the month).
- She rarely gets floppy disks, etc. from other people, but always virus scans them before using them on her computer.
- She annually considers updating her virus scanner to take advantage of new features that may be more compatible with her operating system. However, her operating system and online usage has not changed enough to justify this yet.

LR's Information Protection

- LR stores very little personal, financial and private information on her computer.
- She does not use financial management software.
- She has a second, back-up copy of all data files and keeps them in her personal fireproof and waterproof home safe/lock box.

LR's Computer Use Protection

- LR only has an ID and password registered for her online banking and she always logs off when she has finished banking.
- She always closes her browser and other software when she has finished using them and before someone else uses them.
- She powers down her computer by using "power saver" when not in use for 20 minutes and requires password re-entry to reactivate the computer.
- She always turns off her computer when not in use for an extended period.

LR's Disclosure Protection

- LR only provides general information online, not specific personal information, e.g., she gives her age range as "between 25 and 35 years" rather than her date of birth.
- She does not disclose personal, financial and private information online, and does not file her tax return online.
- She occasionally accesses her online banking website, ensuring that there is an indication it is SSL protected (i.e., the website address begins with HTTPS). She changes her online banking password every six months.
- She occasionally uses the funds transfer feature of her online banking to send birthday money to nieces and nephews, involving e-mail confirmations.
- She does not need to regularly clear her cache, Temporary Internet Files or history files, as there is little that she feels is sensitive.
- She does not use AutoComplete history for electronic forms and passwords. She has configured her browser software to not save user names (IDs) and passwords.
- She does not:
  — Use "MyServices" for creating a custom home page.
  — Have a personal website.
  — Access or use News Groups, Bulletin Boards or Chat Lines.

LR's E-mail Protection

- LR only sends e-mails about family news or routine outreach activities. She never sends e-mails containing her most sensitive personal, financial or private information.
- Her ISP has a spam e-mail scanning service so she rarely gets unwanted e-mails, however any that are received are always deleted without opening them. She never reacts or responds to them.

LR's Information Highway Protection

- LR occasionally buys goods (books, CDs and sending gifts) and services online, including annually renewing her virus scanner and ISP subscriptions with her credit card. She only uses known vendors and websites.
- She does not gamble online.
- She tries to use known, reputable sites for accessing news and information and she does not follow links and pop-up screens that suddenly appear on her screen.
- She has considered installing a personal software firewall but feels this is not necessary due to her infrequent use of dial-up access, her assessment of being low risk and her other protection steps.
- She never uses another computer for personal use other than for research in public places, e.g., the public library.

Resource 6
GLOSSARY OF TECHNICAL TERMS

Applet:
A small Java coded program that is included in the page of a website that works with your browser to connect back to the computer from which the Applet came.

Browser — Microsoft Internet Explorer or Netscape Navigator:
Software that lets you cruise the Internet and search for information, buy goods and access online services, e.g., your bank and bank accounts.

Cache:
Technical capability in your browser that saves previously used web addresses and pages so that they load more quickly when you visit again. The cache also saves web pages of personal, financial and private information you have entered or received, e.g., your bank statement.

Cookie:
A small program or piece of information that is sent to your browser by the web server of a website that you visit. The browser saves the "cookie" and sends back information each time the web server requests it or the browser returns to the website again. Cookies might contain log-in information, your preferences, online shopping information, etc. They cannot act as a virus and search your computer for information.

Defragmentation of Hard Drive:
Technical capability that allows you to "spring clean" your hard drive by re-indexing and organizing your files for more efficient use of the space. Defragmenting also removes all permanently deleted information.

DSL — Digital Subscriber Line:
A high-speed broad bandwidth link over telephone lines, usually available as an ISP service from your telephone company. Also ADSL — Asymmetric DSL and SDSL — Symmetric DSL.

Encryption or Encipherment, and decrypt and decipher:

Encryption (or Encipherment, which has the same meaning) is the act of making original plaintext, readable information unreadable and meaningless by scrambling it such that only the party who is allowed to unscramble (decrypt) it and read it can do so. Encryption is derived from a Greek word meaning "secret writing".

Freeware:

Software and other utilities that can be downloaded and used free of charge. May include trial copies of software from reputable vendors or software developed by others not necessarily for commercial purposes. Can be unstable/unproven and cause your system to crash or be the source of malicious code, e.g., viruses. Also often referred to as Shareware.

Firewall:

Hardware or software, or a combination of both, that segregates the network into parts and provides a secure zone for your computer and any attached networks. Hardware firewalls are essential for "high-risk" Internet users.

IP Address or number — Internet Protocol Address, e.g., 169.142.26.10:

Every computer/server on the Internet has an address as the IP number, which is intended to be unique. Certain numbers are set aside for internal use behind firewalls. Depending on your ISP, you are likely assigned a temporary or dynamic IP address every time you link to the Internet.

ISP — Internet Service Provider:

The enterprise that you use to link to the Internet, e.g., AOL, your cable TV company or telephone company. Could be your employer if you connect through their network.

Hacker:

An individual or entity that attempts to access your computer or personal and financial information without your knowledge and with the intent to read your information, copy it, destroy it or infect you with a virus or equivalent.

LAN — Local Area Network:

A computer network that is within the confines of a relatively small area, i.e., your home or an office building or floor.

Log in, log out, sign in, sign out, enter, exit:

Accessing, and leaving the Internet or a website typically using a personal identifier/name and password.

Malware – see Virus.

Modem – Modulator, DEModulator:
> A devise that connects your computer to a telephone line and lets your computer "talk" over the telephone lines to the Internet.

P3P – Platform for Privacy Preferences:
> Standard machine-readable language and syntax to describe a website's privacy policy.

PEM – Privacy Enhanced Mail:
> Provides privacy through encryption to secure e-mail. Felt generally to be only suitable for small closed groups communicating together.

PIN – Personal Identification Number:
> Generally referred to as the secret code or password that enables you to access your bank and credit cards.

PGP – Pretty Good Privacy:
> Provides authentication through digital signatures and privacy through encryption to secure e-mail using personally generated certificates and keys. Generally felt to be more practical within small groups of users.

Plug-in:
> A small piece of code that adds features to a larger software program. Most commonly used with a browser.

POP – Point Of Presence:
> A city or location away from your home where you can gain access to your ISP through a local or 1-800 telephone number.

POP – Post Office Protocol:
> A mode of operation for e-mail. Your ISP will typically assign you a POP e-mail account.

Proxy Server:
> Sits between your computer and the "real" server you are trying to access/browse to add to security and/or speed response time.

Router:
> A special purpose computer that connects between multiple networks and routes the Internet traffic based on the source and destination address of the information.

S/MIME – Secure Multipurpose Internet Mail Extensions:
Provides authentication through digital signatures and certificates, and privacy through encryption to secure e-mail and attachments. Designed to be inter-operable across e-mail software packages and to work within large numbers of users.

SSL – Secure Socket Layer:
Protocol to encrypt information between the browser and the web server.

Server:
A computer and software package that supports the website you are accessing and works with your browser to complete your request and return the information you need.

Shareware:
See Freeware.

Spam and Spamming:
Unsolicited e-mail, usually an advertisement or chain letter; may include a computer virus.

Spyware:
Trojan horse type program that, while pretending to do one thing, may also be doing something else without your knowledge. For example, while gambling online, the Spyware may be tracking all of your browsing habits and reporting them back to an unknown third party. Spyware is often "installed" when you click on or accept a "pop-up" screen on your computer while online.

TLA:
Three Letter Acronyms.

URL – Uniform Resource Locator:
The address you enter into your browser to reach a website, e.g., http://www.yahoo.ca/

Virus – or worm, Trojan horse:
Often referred to as "malware" or malicious software. Pieces of program code that may do damage to your computer, search your personal, financial or private information and copy and remove your information without your knowledge. Virus infections can occur through disks, over the Internet, from shared software and from e-mail.

Virus Scanner:

Software that is capable of detecting viruses and taking action to ensure that they do not adversely affect your computer and information. Typically have the capability to get regular updates of virus definitions, to run continuously in the background of your computer and to be scheduled to run regularly.

VPN – Virtual Private Network:

The ability to create a secure tunnel through the Internet and other network components, where the user is authenticated as authorized and the information is all encrypted.

WLAN – Wireless Local Area Network:

A computer network that works without wires or physical connections within the confines of a relatively small area, i.e., your home or an office building or floor.

WWW – Worldwide Web:

Used synonymously as the Internet, but incorrectly. The WWW is the total set of interlinked hypertext documents residing on HTTP servers all around the world.

ABOUT THE AUTHORS
ACKNOWLEDGEMENTS

S. J. (JIM) GASTON, FCA

Jim has over 20 years of experience advising major companies and governments on how to manage information technology risks while achieving the benefits that the modern Information Age provides. Dozens of major corporations have implemented Jim's advice on how to gain benefits while at the same time managing risk and providing practical security.

During his career as a senior partner with PriceWaterhouseCoopers and since his recent retirement, Jim has written many books and spoken to a wide variety of audiences in Canada and internationally on all aspects of information technology. His recent publications include *Information Security – Strategies for Successful Management, Mining Data for Knowledge* and *Getting the Right Systems at the Right Price*, published by the CICA. In this publication, Jim has distilled his many years of experience into practical advice that everyone can follow to reduce the risks we all face both on and off the Internet and proactively protect our money, privacy and identity.

PAUL K. WING, FCCA

An independent consultant in information security, privacy and vital infrastructure protection, Paul is a fellow of the Chartered Association of Certified Accounts (UK) with close to 30 years experience in information processing security, audit, control and privacy. Prior to his current career, Paul worked with the Scotiabank for over 20 years. As head of their Information Security, he was involved in designing, securing, auditing and investigating solutions of the Information Age. During this time, banking went from fundamentally a branch operation to electronic service delivery channels of transactions from anywhere in the world at any time, including online.

Paul has led the Security Committees of both the Canadian Bankers (CBA) and Interac Associations, and an electronic commerce focused work group of the Canadian Payment Association (CPA). Paul has had the privilege of representing Canada at both the ISO and the OECD in privacy, electronic authentication and banking cryptography. He is a frequent public speaker and has published several technical articles.

Contact the Authors at protectyourself@rogers.com

Jim and Paul welcome your suggestions, tips and stories. Please e-mail your comments to the authors at: protectyourself@rogers.com

ACKNOWLEDGEMENTS

Jim and Paul thank their family and friends for their encouragement and input, and Jim S, Jorgen, Judy and Dave for the personal time they gave reviewing and contributing valuable ideas to the early drafts of the manuscript. We are particularly grateful to Beverley Edwards for writing a spirited Foreword and to our editor Kathleen Aldridge, B.A., Dip.Ed. for her dedication, help and advice. And finally, we thank the professionals we worked with at the Canadian Institute of Chartered Accountants for their encouragement and support, in particular Tracey Jones-Inch who designed the cover and the interior of the book, Maggie Tyson, Manager — Editorial Development, and Peter J. Hoult, CA, Director of Information and Productivity Resources.

Jim thanks his co-author Paul for all the learning he provided while writing this book and for his unfailing patience in responding to his many questions and listening to his point of view.

Paul thanks Jim for providing him with the opportunity to undertake this project and fulfill a lifetime ambition. Paul dedicates his work to his family, and to Sgt. Pepper and Captain Fantastic for their inspiration.